At Issue

Is Iran a Threat to Global Security?

Other books in the At Issue series:

At Issue

Is Iran a Threat to Global Security?

Julia Bauder, Book Editor

GREENHAVEN PRESS
An imprint of Thomson Gale, a part of The Thomson Corporation

THOMSON
—————✳————— ™
GALE

Detroit • New York • San Francisco • New Haven, Conn. • Waterville, Maine • London • Munich

THOMSON
★ ™
GALE

Bonnie Szumski, *Publisher*
Helen Cothran, *Managing Editor*

© 2006 Thomson Gale, a part of The Thomson Corporation.

Thomson and Star logo are trademarks and Gale and Greenhaven Press are registered trademarks used herein under license.

For more information, contact: Greenhaven Press
27500 Drake Rd.
Farmington Hills, MI 48331-3535
Or you can visit our Internet site at http://www.gale.com

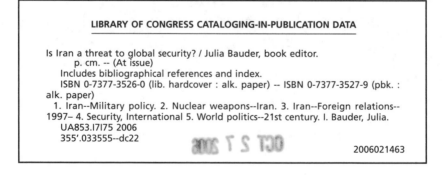

LIBRARY OF CONGRESS CATALOGING-IN-PUBLICATION DATA

Is Iran a threat to global security? / Julia Bauder, book editor.
    p. cm. -- (At issue)
    Includes bibliographical references and index.
    ISBN 0-7377-3526-0 (lib. hardcover : alk. paper) -- ISBN 0-7377-3527-9 (pbk. : alk. paper)
    1. Iran--Military policy. 2. Nuclear weapons--Iran. 3. Iran--Foreign relations-- 1997– 4. Security, International 5. World politics--21st century. I. Bauder, Julia.
    UA853.I7I75 2006
    355'.033555--dc22
                                                            2006021463

Printed in the United States of America
10 9 8 7 6 5 4 3 2 1

Contents

Introduction

Worries about the threat that Iran could pose to global security are not new. The country has a long history of troubled relationships with the rest of the world, going back to ancient times when Iran—then called Persia—was a great power that ruled much of the Middle East and southwestern Asia. In recent years, however, these worries have taken on a greater urgency, as Iran seems increasingly likely to acquire nuclear weapons, giving the country the ability to menace other countries in a way that it never could before.

The Iranians, on the other hand, are equally worried about the rest of the world's threat to their own security—worries that are firmly rooted in the history of the relationships between Iran and the world's other powers. Turks and Russians tore off large pieces of Iranian territory for themselves between the sixteenth and nineteenth centuries. During World War I, Turkey, Great Britain, and Russia all invaded neutral Iran, and Russia and Great Britain repeated their invasions in World War II. Then in 1953 the United States and Great Britain backed a coup to overthrow the democratically elected government of Iran and replace it with a Western-friendly autocratic monarchy under Shah Mohammad Reza Pahlavi, in order to protect the two Western nations' profits from the production and sale of Iranian oil.

Iran struck back against the Western powers in 1979, when the Iranian people overthrew the shah's government and replaced it with an Islamic republic under Ayatollah Ruhollah Khomeini. As part of this Islamic Revolution, fifty-two American citizens were taken hostage in the American embassy in Tehran by students affiliated with the revolutionary government. The hostage-taking was meant to protest the U.S. decision to allow the shah, who had advanced cancer, to enter the United States to receive treatment. The students said that the hostages would not be released until the shah was turned over to the new government of Iran. Eventually the shah died and, 444 days after they were taken hostage, the Americans were released, but the incident had lasting effects on relations between Iran and the United States. During the hostage crisis the American government severed relations with Iran, froze Iranian assets in the United States, and imposed severe economic sanctions on the country, which had previously had a strong trading relationship with the United States. Moreover, when Iraq invaded Iran in 1980 the United States threw its support behind Iraq. For the most part these actions were not reversed when the hostages were freed; in fact, the United States still does not have any embassies or consulates in Iran.

The new Iranian government's active support of Islamic militant groups in other countries, particularly Hizballah in Lebanon, also brought it into conflict with the West. In 1983 Hizballah sent a truck bomb into the U.S. Marines barracks in Beirut, Lebanon, killing 241 American service members. Fifty-eight French paratroopers were also killed in a similar bombing that happened at the same time. These attacks only deepened the rift between the West and Iran.

The election of a moderate, reformist president, Mohammad Khatami, in 1997 raised hopes for a better relationship between Iran and the rest of the world, but conservative factions in the government succeeded in blocking many of Khatami's reforms. Iran's nuclear program, which had worried the West since the early 1980s, continued—although the Iranians insisted that they wanted only to build nuclear power plants, not nuclear weapons—and the United States continued to take a hard line with Iran. President George W. Bush even designated it part of the "Axis of Evil" in January 2002.

During 2002 and 2003 more information emerged about the extent of Iran's nuclear program, showing that the program was more advanced than many had believed. In June 2003 the International Atomic Energy Agency, the world's nuclear watchdog, ruled that Iran was in violation of the Nuclear Non-Proliferation Treaty (NPT). The so-called EU3—European Union members Great Britain, France, and Germany—opened negotiations with Iran about scaling back or stopping its program and coming into compliance with the NPT, but these negotiations dragged out, with both sides making some concessions but with no overall agreement in sight.

Then, in the summer of 2005 a new president was elected in Iran: Mahmoud Ahmadinejad, a fundamentalist hard-liner who took a much more confrontational stand with the West and who threw his full support behind Iran's nuclear program. Despite the efforts of Britain, France, and Germany to negotiate an end to that program, the nuclear talks continued to show little progress and have been suspended on several occasions. The apparent failure of these negotiations leaves the rest of the world's countries with many difficult decisions to make. Is it possible that these negotiations could still succeed in the future? If not, is Iran's nuclear program truly a threat that must be eliminated, or can the world safely tolerate an Iran armed with nuclear weapons? If a nuclear-armed Iran cannot be tolerated, what should be done to prevent the country's nuclear program from progressing any further? These are questions whose answers are far from clear. The authors of the viewpoints in *At Issue: Is Iran a Threat to Global Security?* debate these issues.

1

Iran Is a Major Threat to Global Security

Michael A. Ledeen

Michael A. Ledeen is a resident scholar in American foreign policy with the American Enterprise Institute, a conservative Washington, D.C., think tank. He is the author of several books, including The War Against the Terror Masters: Why It Happened, Where We Are Now, How We'll Win.

Iran's nuclear program and its support of terrorists pose a serious threat to the United States, Israel, and other Western countries. The Iranian government has made this threat clear through both its words—including explicit threats to destroy Israel and the United States—and its actions, such as aiding militant groups in Iraq. Iran has also provided safe haven and assistance to al Qaeda leaders, who have used that assistance to plan and carry out terrorist attacks around the world. Yet despite these clear indications, Western countries have done little about the danger from Iran.

M irabile dictu, as they used to say before Dante—all of a sudden everyone has noticed that Iran really wants the destruction of Israel. "What took them so long?" you may well ask (as I certainly do). . . . On September 28, [2005,] there was a monster parade in Tehran featuring the country's armed forces. One of the high points of the parade was a collection of the Shahab 3 missiles, the ones designed to carry nuclear warheads, and they were adorned with catchy slogans like "The Zionist regime [Israel] must be destroyed," and "Death to America."

Four military attaches walked out in protest: the French, the Italian, the Greek and the Polish. But that was about it. The Western world had made its point by bravely abandoning the parade grounds. I didn't see any nasty condemnation of the warmongers in Tehran, I don't remember even the toothless jaws of the United Nations condemning the Islamic republic [Iran], and I certainly saw nothing vaguely resembling an effective policy to bring down the mullahs before they go for our exposed veins and arteries, even though Her Majesty's Government [of Britain] had long been aware that the Iranian Revolutionary Guards were arming, training, funding, and guiding terrorists from Khuzestan [in southwestern Iran] across the Shatt-al-Arab into southern Iraq, and that Iranian-intelligence officers were openly advocating the creation of an Islamic republic in the Shiite south, along Khomeinist lines.

Iran Supports Terrorists in Iraq

Indeed, on September 12 [2005,] *Al Sharq Al Awsat* [an Arabic newspaper published in London] reported that "officials from the Revolutionary Guard have recently met with leaders of Ansar al Islam [a radical Islamic terrorist group] and the Jihad organizations . . . near the Iranian-Iraq borders. They discussed the acceleration of military operations against the British forces in the south of Iraq." It didn't take long to confirm this information. Richard Beeston of the London *Times* wrote on the 20th that the Brits had reason to believe that new attacks against British forces in southern Iraq "[are] being orchestrated with weapons and encouragement from Iran."

By October 9, Con Coughlin was writing in the London *Telegraph* that a British diplomat traveling from Baghdad to London "unwittingly strayed from his brief and started laying into the Iranians with a gusto not seen in the British diplomatic service for decades. The Iranians, said the diplomat, were colluding with Sunni Muslim insurgent groups in southern Iraq. . . ."

Notice that he said "Sunni." We already knew about Shiite, as in Moqtadah al Sadr [a Shiite cleric and anti-American militia leader], and SCIRI's [Supreme Council of Islamic Revolution in Iraq] Badr Brigades, most of whom were trained in Iran over the past two decades. If any of you has any friends over at CIA [the U.S. Central Intelligence Agency] (my last buddy left a few weeks ago), point it out to them, please.

The Iranian people suffer, demonstrate, protest, and die, but not a single Western country has come up with a serious Iran policy.

Iran Supports Terrorists in the United States

While you're at it, you might also point out that one of Iran's favorite terrorist organizations, Islamic Jihad, is having its moment in court in south Florida, and an interesting bit of information unexpectedly crept into the record. Mr. Kerry Myers, an FBI [Federal Bureau of Investigation] agent, was asked by the defense attorney whether Islamic Jihad had done any mean things outside Israel, Gaza, or the West Bank (as if terrorism against Israelis doesn't count, you know). Myers pointed out that IJ had threatened the United States. The attorney asked if there had ever been an actual action by IJ. And

Myers burst out with "I can tell you there was a plot to commit terrorist acts in the United States. It was interdicted, I believe."

I have long since lost track of how many Iranian U.N. "diplomats" have been tossed out of this country after being caught photographing New York tunnels, bridges, subway stations, and monuments.

But nobody does anything to take the terror war to the Iranians. The Iranian people suffer, demonstrate, protest, and die, but not a single Western country has come up with a serious Iran policy. . . .

Iran Supports Terrorists in Europe

Meanwhile, *Cicero* magazine in Germany has published two long articles that confirm what I have long said, namely that al Qaeda receives enormous support from Iran. According to the BKA, Germany's FBI, Iran "provided [Abu Musab al-]Zarqawi with logistical support on the part of the state." Like other al Qaeda leaders, Zarqawi went from Afghanistan to Iran, and set up his training camps and safe houses in Zahedan, Isfahan, and Tehran. He was the driving force behind the Madrid bombings and those in Bali, and Iranian support was given throughout. After all, according to the *Cicero* article, the coordination of jihadi groups from all over the world is coordinated from Iran. "They live in secure housing of the Revolutionary Guards in and around Tehran. 'This is not detention or house arrest,' concludes a high-ranking secret-service employee. 'They come and go as they please.'"

According to the Germans (echoed by the celebrated Spanish judge, Balthazar Garzon), the jihadis are organizing attacks against the West, including the United States. The newspapers are full of snapshots of the jihad-to-be.

- In France, there are reports that an al Qaeda cell has smuggled two surface-to-air missiles into the country. And *Al Watan*, an often reliable Saudi newspaper, said that French counter terrorist forces had found a deadly poison in the home of one of the cell members.

- In Holland, seven presumed Islamic terrorists were arrested in the Hague after an armed struggle.

- Back in July [2005], a terror network in the Hague was dismantled, leading to the discovery of documents showing deals for night-vision goggles, helicopters, and over one million gas masks, apparently destined for Chechen terrorists.

- Four young men, described as "of Mid-Eastern descent and deeply devout Muslims," were arrested in Copenhagen and charged with planning a suicide terrorist attack in the near future against the United States or British embassy in Sarajevo. Two more men were arrested the next day, prompting the BBC [British Broadcasting Corporation], ever concerned to debunk the very idea that we might be at war with jihadis, noted that "the case comes at a time when Denmark is experiencing severe problems in relations with its Muslim community," devoted four paragraphs to a discussion of caricatures of the prophet Mohammed in a Danish paper, and concludes brightly with "it is in this atmosphere that the arrest of six, 16–20-year old Muslims on what appears so far at least to be very flimsy evidence may serve to further alienate the Muslim community of Denmark."

- On October 16, [2005,] the London *Times* reported that the British government had found that Zarqawi has created a new group in Britain that is recruiting fighters for the jihad in Iraq, and that returning jihadis may be planning attacks.

- In Italy, there are continuing reports of close working relations between Italian mafias, especially the Neapolitan *camorra*, and al Qaeda.

This is what we're up against. It is a frenetic network of fanatical terrorists, supported by a group of mad mullahs hell-bent on our destruction. Forget about the microanalysis of the Iraqi 'insurgency.' This is not primarily a war conducted by angry Baathist remnants of Saddam's bloody regime; it's much bigger than that, and the epicenter of the whole thing is in Tehran, and its ideology is brutally enunciated by [Iranian president Mahmoud] Ahmadi Nezhad.

Britain, France, and Italy are at least expelling some of the jihadis, along with some of the most fanatical religious leaders. We are not, so far as one can see, doing even that. And we are certainly not taking any of the obvious, rational, and thoroughly justifiable steps to provide political and economic support to the most potent enemies of the world's most dangerous terrorist regime: the Iranian people.

Sooner or later, one of these many schemes will succeed, and we will have a new version of September 11th. Perhaps only then will our dithering leaders resume fighting the war against terror, a war currently limited, to their shame, to a defensive struggle within the boundaries of Iraq, while they move against us on a global scale.

Faster, please.

2

Iran Is Not a Major Threat to Global Security

Ray Takeyh

Ray Takeyh is a senior fellow at the Council on Foreign Relations. He is also the author, with Nikolas K. Gvosdev, of The Receding Shadow of the Prophet: The Rise and Fall of Radical Political Islam.

Iran is not the threat to global security that it may have been in the past. Its rulers have matured since the 1979 revolution, and Iran's international goals now have more to do with protecting its self-interest than with encouraging Islamic revolutions in other countries. Iran's nuclear program is worrisome, but it is unlikely that Iran will substantially alter its generally peaceful foreign policy any time soon.

[The September 2005] vote by the International Atomic Energy Agency branding Iran in breach of its Nuclear Non-Proliferation Treaty (NPT) commitments has given impetus to the United States to call for the referral of Iran to the UN Security Council. Tehran is adamant that it wants nuclear power for generating electricity. Yet, Washington policymakers and their European counterparts subtly argue that Iran's previous treaty violations indicate a more sinister motive to subvert its neighbors and export its Islamic revolution.

Such alarmism overlooks Iran's realities. In the past decade, a fundamental shift in Iran's international orientation has enshrined national interest calculations as the defining factor in its approach to the world. Irrespective of the balance of power between conservatives and reformers, Iran's foreign policy is driven by fixed principles that are shared by all of its political elites.

The intense factional struggles that have plagued the clerical state during the past decade obscure the emergence of a consensus foreign policy. Under Supreme Leader Ayatollah Ali Khamenei, a loose coalition emerged around the notion that Iran cannot remain isolated in the global order.

By cultivating favorable relations with key international actors such as China, Russia, and the European Union, Tehran has sought to craft its own "coalition of willing" and prevent the US from multilateralizing its coercive approach to Iran. Although the Islamic Republic continues its inflammatory support for terrorist organizations battling Israel and is pressing ahead with its nuclear program, its foreign policy is no longer that of a revolutionary state.

This perspective will survive Iran's latest leadership transition. The demographic complexion of the regime's rulers is changing. As Iran's revolution matures and those politicians who were present at the creation of the Islamic Republic gradually recede from the scene, a more austere and dogmatic generation is beginning to take over the reins of power. In response to Iran's manifold problems ... President Mahmoud Ahmadinejad and his cabinet frequently criticize their elders' passivity in imposing Islamic strictures and for the rampant corruption that has engulfed the state. They are determined to reverse the social and cultural freedoms of the reformist period and to institute egalitarian economic policies.

On foreign policy issues, however, the new president has stayed well within the parameters of Iran's prevailing international policy. In his August [2005] address to the parliament, Mr. Ahmadinejad echoed the existing consensus, noting the importance of constructive relations with "the Islamic world, the Persian Gulf region, the Caspian Sea region, Central Asia, the Pacific area, and Europe." Moreover, the most important voice on foreign policy matters, . . . [the] head of the Supreme National Security Council, Ali Larijani, has reiterated these same themes.

Although the assertive nationalists who have taken command of Iran's executive branch have dispensed with their predecessor's "dialogue of civilizations" rhetoric, and display a marked indifference to reestablishment of relations with America, they are loath to jeopardize the successful multilateral détente that was the singular achievement of the reformist era.

All this is not to suggest that the current negotiations between Iran and the EU-3 (France, Britain, and Germany) designed to resolve the nuclear stalemate will resume. More than two years of talks have failed to bridge the essential differences.

Grand Ayatollah Ruhollah Khomeini's disciples have long abandoned the mission of exporting the revolution, supplanting it with conventional measures of the national interest.

Iran continues to assert its right under the NPT to enrich uranium and has accepted an intrusive inspection regime, while the Europeans insist that Iran must atone for its previous treaty violations by permanently suspending such activities. Ultimately, it appears impossible to reconcile these positions.

It is important to note, however, that the divergence between the European and Iranian perspective predated the rise of Ahmadinejad. This highlights a worrisome convergence in Iranian political thought over the past two years: Somehow—as a result of misguided nationalism or a genuine sense of necessity—mastery of the nuclear fuel cycle has become a sine qua non of modern Iranian politics.

Its nuclear ambitions will continue to irritate the international community, but the days when Iran wantonly sought to undermine established authority in the name of Islamic salvation are over. Grand Ayatollah Ruhollah Khomeini's disciples have long abandoned the mission of exporting the revolution, supplanting it with conventional measures of the national interest.

Despite the chorus of concern, Iran's president has demonstrated no interest in substantially altering the contours of Iran's international policy—nor has the country's ultimate authority, the Supreme Leader. To be sure, the new president's well-honed reactionary instincts will be felt by his hapless constituents as he proceeds to restrict their political and social prerogatives.

But the notion that Iran's foreign policy is entering a new radical state is yet another misreading of the Islamic Republic and its many paradoxes.

3

Iran's Nuclear Program Is a Serious Threat to Israel

Charles Krauthammer

Charles Krauthammer is an award-winning columnist for the Washington Post.

Iran and its nuclear program pose a life-or-death threat to Israel. The Iranian president has publicly called for Israel to be destroyed, and the possession of nuclear weapons would allow Iran to accomplish this destruction. Moreover, Shiite Muslims believe that there will be a bloody apocalypse at the end of time, and the Iranian president and some others believe that the end of time is near. This belief will make Iran very difficult to deter with threats of retaliation, since its leaders may see a nuclear war as helping to hasten the end and to bring the Islamic messiah back more quickly. A government led by people who hold such beliefs should not be allowed to acquire nuclear weapons.

Lest you get carried away with good news from Iraq [regarding progress toward the war's goals], consider what's happening next door in Iran. The wild pronouncements of the Iranian president, Mahmoud Ahmadinejad, have gotten sporadic press ever since he called for Israel to be wiped off the map. He subsequently amended himself to say that Israel should simply be extirpated from the Middle East map and moved to some German or Austrian province. Perhaps near the site of an old extermination camp?

Iranian Anti-Semitism

Except that there were no such camps, indeed no Holocaust at all, says Ahmadinejad. Nothing but "myth," a "legend" that was "fabricated . . . under the name 'Massacre of the Jews.'" This brought the usual reaction from European and American officials, who, with Churchillian rage and power, called these statements unacceptable. That something serious might accrue to Iran for this—say, expulsion from the United Nations for violating its most basic principle by advocating the outright eradication of a member state—is, of course, out of the question.

To be sure, Holocaust denial and calls for Israel's destruction are commonplace in the Middle East. They can be seen every day on Hezbollah TV, in Syrian media, in Egyptian editorials appearing in semiofficial newspapers. But none of these aspiring mass murderers are on the verge of acquiring nuclear weapons that could do in one afternoon what it took Hitler six years to do: destroy an entire Jewish civilization and extinguish 6 million souls.

Everyone knows where Iran's nuclear weapons will be aimed. Everyone knows they will be put on Shahab rockets, which have been modified so that they can reach Israel. And everyone knows that if the button is ever pushed, it will be the end of Israel.

The president of a country about to go nuclear is a confirmed believer in the coming apocalypse.

Belief in the Apocalypse

But it gets worse. The president of a country about to go nuclear is a confirmed believer in the coming apocalypse. Like

Judaism and Christianity, Shiite Islam has its own version of the messianic return—the reappearance of the Twelfth Imam. The more devout believers in Iran pray at the Jamkaran mosque, which houses a well from which, some believe, he will emerge.

When Ahmadinejad unexpectedly won the presidential elections, he immediately gave $17 million of government funds to the shrine. [In November 2005,] Ahmadinejad said publicly that the main mission of the Islamic Revolution is to pave the way for the reappearance of the Twelfth Imam.

And as in some versions of fundamentalist Christianity, the second coming will be accompanied by the usual trials and tribulations, death and destruction. Iranian journalist Hossein Bastani reported Ahmadinejad saying in official meetings that the hidden imam will reappear in two years [by 2007].

So a Holocaust-denying, virulently anti-Semitic, aspiring genocidist, on the verge of acquiring weapons of the apocalypse, believes that the end is not only near but nearer than the next American presidential election. . . . This kind of man would have, to put it gently, less inhibition about starting Armageddon than a normal person. Indeed, with millennial bliss pending, he would have positive incentive to, as they say in Jewish eschatology, hasten the end.

To be sure, there are such madmen among the other monotheisms. The Temple Mount Faithful in Israel would like the al-Aqsa mosque on Jerusalem's Temple Mount destroyed to make way for the third Jewish Temple and the messianic era. The difference with Iran, however, is that there are all of about 50 of these nuts in Israel, and none of them is president.

The closest we've come to a messianically inclined leader in America was a secretary of the interior who [in 1981], when asked about his stewardship of the environment, told Congress: "I do not know how many future generations we can count on before the Lord returns; whatever it is we have to manage with a skill to leave the resources needed for future generations." But James Watt's domain was the forest, and his weapon of choice was the chainsaw. He was not in charge of nuclear weapons to be placed on missiles that are paraded through the streets with, literally, Israel's name on them. (They are adorned with banners reading "Israel must be wiped off the map.") It gets worse. After his U.N. speech in September [2005], Ahmadinejad was caught on videotape telling a cleric that during the speech an aura, a halo, appeared around his head right on the podium of the General Assembly. "I felt the atmosphere suddenly change. And for those 27 or 28 minutes, the leaders of the world did not blink. . . . It seemed as if a hand was holding them there, and it opened their eyes to receive the message from the Islamic Republic."

Negotiations to deny this certifiable lunatic genocidal weapons have been going nowhere. Everyone knows they will go nowhere. And no one will do anything about it.

Iran's Nuclear Program Is Not a Threat to Israel

Carl Coon

Carl Coon was a member of the U.S. Foreign Service from 1947 through 1985 and spent three of those years as ambassador to Nepal. He is the author of two books, including One Planet, One People: Beyond "Us vs. Them."

Iran's nuclear program is not a threat to Israel because Iran has no intention of launching a nuclear attack on that country. The Iranian regime is not suicidal, and it will not want to risk a nuclear counterattack from Israel. Iran merely wants to counter Israel's nuclear deterrent with one of its own. This will put Iran and Israel into a Mutually Assured Destruction (MAD) scenario, which, as the Cold War proved, can provide a stable equilibrium.

On December 11 [2005], the London *Times* reported that the Israelis are increasingly concerned that the Iranians will soon reach the point of no return in their effort to develop a nuclear weapons capability, and are gearing up for military action . . . that will eliminate the threat for years to come. The Israeli Foreign Minister denied the report, but in my opinion the denial lacks plausibility. . . .

The report can be seen as another ploy to bring the Iranians in line, and no doubt that is one reason it has appeared at this time. But I think we have to assume there is

Carl Coon, "Madness in the Middle East, an Iranian Nuke?" *Progressive Humanism*, December 12, 2005. Reproduced by permission.

more to it than bluff. The Iranians have solid reasons for wanting to develop at least a moderate nuclear weapons capability and the Israelis have sound reasons for wanting to stop them. Conventional wisdom in Washington may be that the Iranians must be stopped, but before we go too far down that road we need to consider all the relevant angles and weigh the consequences of various courses of action. And we need to do it now, if the report is right in stating that the Israelis are operating on a very short fuse.

Why Iran Wants Nuclear Weapons

Of course the Iranians lie when they say they only want power, not nukes. Iran feels compelled to develop a nuclear weapons capability for somewhat the same reasons that impelled the USSR to do so fifty-odd years ago, and more recently propelled first India and then Pakistan into the nuclear club. Iran is doing what every Arab state would like to do if it could: react to the Israeli nuclear weapons capability by developing its own deterrent. It is MAD all over again, mutually assured destruction, equilibrium through balance of terror.

An Iranian nuclear deterrent could end up being a stabilizing force in the troubled cauldron of Middle Eastern interstate relations.

Iran has no intention of using whatever nukes it may develop to attack Israel. It would have to reckon with the possibility that even if it could survive an Israeli counterattack, the USA might react, and destroy Iran with its much larger nuclear arsenal. Whether we would respond this way or not, the mere possibility would deter Iran from initiating an attack on Israel. The familiar principle of judging by capability, not stated intentions, would apply. The Iranians are not suicidal.

What the Iranians want is the capability to inflict unacceptable damage on Israel in the expectation that that capability would alter Israel's behavior. Just as the Iranians would be deterred by the possibility, not probability, of a US response, so Israel would be deterred by a possibility (not a probability) of an Iranian nuclear attack. The Iranian deterrent need be neither large nor particularly sophisticated for MAD to work, for Israel's small size makes it inherently vulnerable.

In this sense an Iranian nuclear deterrent could end up being a stabilizing force in the troubled cauldron of Middle Eastern interstate relations. Of course the Israelis won't see it that way, nor will many Americans. But we need to bear in mind that Iran will never in the foreseeable future be a direct threat to our own survival, and that what we are really dealing with is more a problem of a realignment of the balance of forces in the Middle East than an existential threat to Israel's existence.

The Dangers of an Israeli Preemptive Attack

If Israel does attack . . . we will be well and truly on the spot. Iran is not Iraq in 1981. This will not be a pushover like the Osirak caper.[1] The Iranians have been getting ready for such an attack for quite a while now, and I suspect their counterintelligence is pretty good. So what do we do if the Israeli attack bogs down; support the Israelis with our own forces? There still may be a neocon [new conservative Republican] or two in high places in Washington who would favor this, but a moment's reflection will convince the rest of us it would be lunacy. And it would be insane even if we limited our support to air power and logistics. Russia and China would each have their own reasons to extend at least diplomatic support to the Iranians and perhaps more, leading to a crisis situation that could damage our important interests in Moscow and Beijing for years and even decades to come.

1. In 1981 the Israeli air force destroyed a nuclear reactor that Iraq was building at Osirak.

Which way would [Pakistani president Pervez] Musharraf jump? Or the EU [European Union]? And so on. The list of migraines we would incur is almost endless.

I conclude that if our government has even a modicum of concern left for our country's welfare it will quietly but firmly tell the Israelis, right now, to knock it off. After all, this adventure could be a disaster for Israel as well. And what are friends for?

Looking a bit farther ahead, I hope we won't fall on our sword over this Iranian nuclear issue. It is one of many major interests we have in the region. We cannot win them all. In the long run, there has to be an international rule of law that governs nukes everywhere. Pending that, MADness is likely to reign, in the Middle East as elsewhere.

5

Israel Is a Threat to the Islamic World

Mahmoud Ahmadinejad

Mahmoud Ahmadinejad is the president of Iran.

The existence of Israel is a provocation to the Islamic world. Israel's creation was a continuation of the centuries-long war between the West and Islamic countries, and the West intends to use its foothold in Israel to expand its control over the rest of the Islamic world. It is unacceptable for such an enemy foothold to exist in the middle of the Islamic territories; therefore, Israel must be removed. Such a goal may seem difficult to achieve, but if Islamic countries band together and do not let the West pressure them into individually recognizing and making peace with Israel it is possible.

[Editor's Note: The following introduction was provided by the Middle East Media Research Institute (MEMRI), who translated this speech.]

In advance of Iran's Jerusalem Day, which was established by Ayatollah [Ruhollah] Khomeini and is marked annually on the fourth Friday of the month of Ramadan, the "World without Zionism" conference was held in Tehran.

"Iranian President at Tehran Conference: 'Very Soon, This Stain of Disgrace [i.e., Israel] Will Be Purged from the Center of the Islamic World—and This Is Attainable,'" www.memri.org, no. 1013, October 28, 2005. Reproduced by permission.

At the conference, Iranian President Mahmoud Ahmadinejad spoke to the representatives of [Muslim militant groups] Hamas and Islamic Jihad, members of the Society for the Defense of the Palestinian Nation, and members of the Islamic Students Union, and an audience of hundreds of students. . . .

The Iranian Students News Agency (ISNA) published the full text of Ahmadinejad's speech. The following is a translation of excerpts from ISNA's report and from the speech.

"Prior to his statement, Ahmadinejad said that if you plan to chant the slogan 'Death to Israel,' say it in the right and complete way.

"The president warned the leaders of the Islamic world that they should be wary of Fitna [civil strife]: 'If someone is under the pressure of hegemonic power [i.e., the West] and misunderstands something is wrong or he is naïve, or he is an egotist and his hedonism leads him to recognize the Zionist regime—he should know that he will burn in the fire of the Islamic Ummah [nation]. . . .'

"Ahmadinejad articulated the real meaning of Zionism: '. . . We must see what the real story of Palestine is. . . . The establishment of the regime that is occupying Jerusalem was a very grave move by the hegemonic and arrogant system [i.e., the West] against the Islamic world. We are in the process of an historical war between the World of Arrogance [i.e., the West] and the Islamic world, and this war has been going on for hundreds of years.

"'In this historical war, the situation at the fronts has changed many times. During some periods, the Muslims were the victors and were very active, and looked forward, and the World of Arrogance was in retreat.

"'Unfortunately, in the past 300 years, the Islamic world has been in retreat vis-à-vis the World of Arrogance. . . . During the period of the last 100 years, the [walls of the] world of Islam were destroyed and the World of Arrogance turned the regime occupying Jerusalem into a bridge for its dominance over the Islamic world. . . .

"'This occupying country [i.e., Israel] is in fact a front of the World of Arrogance in the heart of the Islamic world. They have in fact built a bastion [Israel] from which they can expand their rule to the entire Islamic world. . . . This means that the current war in Palestine is the front line of the Islamic world against the World of Arrogance, and will determine the fate of Palestine for centuries to come.

"'Today the Palestinian nation stands against the hegemonic system as the representative of the Islamic Ummah [nation]. Thanks to God, since the Palestinian people adopted the Islamic war and the Islamic goals, and since their struggle has become Islamic in its attitude and orientation, we have been witnessing the progress and success of the Palestinian people.'

"Ahmadinejad said: 'The issue of this [World without Zionism] conference is very valuable. In this very grave war, many people are trying to scatter grains of desperation and hopelessness regarding the struggle between the Islamic world and the front of the infidels, and in their hearts they want to empty the Islamic world.

"'. . . They [ask]: "Is it possible for us to witness a world without America and Zionism?" But you had best know that this slogan and this goal are attainable, and surely can be achieved. . . .

"'When the dear Imam [Khomeini] said that [Shah's] regime must go, and that we demand a world without dependent governments, many people who claimed to have political and other knowledge [asked], "Is it possible [that the Shah's regime can be toppled]?"

"'That day, when Imam [Khomeini] began his movement, all the powers supported [the Shah's] corrupt regime . . . and said it was not possible. However, our nation stood firm, and by now we have, for 27 years, been living without a government dependent on America. Imam [Khomeni] said: "The rule of the East [U.S.S.R.] and of the West [U.S.] should be ended." But the weak people who saw only the tiny world near them did not believe it.

"'Nobody believed that we would one day witness the collapse of the Eastern Imperialism [i.e., the U.S.S.R], and said it was an iron regime. But in our short lifetime we have witnessed how this regime collapsed in such a way that we must look for it in libraries, and we can find no literature about it.

"'Imam [Khomeini] said that Saddam [Hussein] must go, and that he would be humiliated in a way that was unprecedented. And what do you see today? A man who, 10 years ago, spoke as proudly as if he would live for eternity is today chained by the feet, and is now being tried in his own country. . . .

"'Imam [Khomeini] said: 'This regime that is occupying Qods [Jerusalem] must be eliminated from the pages of history.' This sentence is very wise. The issue of Palestine is not an issue on which we can compromise.

"'Is it possible that an [Islamic] front allows another front [i.e., country] to arise in its [own] heart? This means defeat, and he who accepts the existence of this regime [i.e., Israel] in fact signs the defeat of the Islamic world.

"'In his battle against the World of Arrogance, our dear Imam [Khomeini] set the regime occupying Qods [Jerusalem] as the target of his fight.

"'I do not doubt that the new wave which has begun in our dear Palestine and which today we are also witnessing in the Islamic world is a wave of morality which has spread all over the Islamic world. Very soon, this stain of disgrace [i.e., Israel] will be purged from the center of the Islamic world—and this is attainable.

"'But we must be wary of Fitna. For more than 50 years, the World of Arrogance has tried to give recognition to the existence of this falsified regime [Israel]. With its first steps, and then with further steps, it has tried hard in this direction to stabilize it.

"'Regrettably, 27 or 28 years ago . . . one of the countries of the first line [i.e., Egypt] made this failure [of recognizing Israel]—and we still hope that they will correct it.

"'Lately we have new Fitna underway. . . . With the forced evacuation [of Gaza] that was imposed by the Palestinian people, they [the Israelis] evacuated only a corner. [Israel] declared this as the final victory and, on the pretext of evacuating Gaza and establishing a Palestinian government, tried to put an end to the hopes of the Palestinians.

"'Today, [Israel] seeks, satanically and deceitfully, to gain control of the front of war. It is trying to influence the Palestinian groups in Palestine so as to preoccupy them with political issues and jobs—so that they relinquish the Palestinian cause that determines their destiny, and come into conflict with each other.

"'On the pretext of goodwill, they [Israel] intended, by evacuating the Gaza strip, to gain recognition of its corrupt regime by some Islamic states. I very much hope, and ask God, that the Palestinian people and the dear Palestinian groups will be wary of this Fitna.

The Islamic people cannot allow this historical enemy [Israel] to exist in the heart of the Islamic world.

"'The issue of Palestine is by no means over, and will end only when all of Palestine will have a government belonging to the Palestinian people. The refugees must return to their homes, and there must be a government that has come to power by the will of the [Palestinian] people. And, of course those [i.e., the Jews] who came to this country from far away to plunder it have no right to decide anything for the [Palestinian] people.

"'I hope that the Palestinians will maintain their wariness and intelligence, much as they have pursued their battles in the past 10 years. This will be a short period, and if we pass through it successfully, the process of the elimination of the Zionist regime will be smooth and simple.

"'I warn all the leaders of the Islamic world to be wary of Fitna: If someone is under the pressure of hegemonic power [i.e., the West] and understands that something is wrong, or he is naïve, or he is an egotist and his hedonism leads him to recognize the Zionist regime—he should know that he will burn in the fire of the Islamic Ummah [nation]. . . .

"'The people who sit in closed rooms cannot decide on this matter. The Islamic people cannot allow this historical enemy [Israel] to exist in the heart of the Islamic world.

"'Oh dear people, look at this global arena. By whom are we confronted? We have to understand the depth of the disgrace of the enemy, until our holy hatred expands continuously and strikes like a wave.'"

6

Iran Is Interfering with Efforts to Build a Stable Iraq

Peter Brookes

Peter Brookes is a Senior Fellow for National Security Affairs at the Heritage Foundation, a conservative Washington, D.C., think tank. He is also the author of the book A Devil's Triangle: Terrorism, Weapons of Mass Destruction and Rogue States.

While Iran's nuclear program is a problem for the United States, the most immediate threat from Iran is its support of terrorists in Iraq. Iran stands to gain a great deal of influence over Iraq, and possibly some Iraqi territory, if the United States fails to build a stable government there. Moreover, Iran does not want American troops to be stationed long-term on both their eastern and western borders, in Afghanistan and Iraq, respectively. The danger from Iran in Iraq is not merely theoretical; the U.S. Army has found Iranian-made weapons in the country. The United States must respond forcefully to Iran's meddling in Iraq with economic sanctions or with military force if necessary.

Iran is becoming a foreign-policy problem of almost immeasurable proportions—from its nuclear-weapons brinkmanship to its feverish support of Islamic fundamentalism and international terrorism.

Peter Brookes, "Facing the Facts About Iran," www.heritage.org, August 23, 2005.

But Tehran's most proximate—and often overlooked—threat to American interests is its attempts to destabilize Iraq by supporting and fomenting its own insurgency against Coalition and Iraqi forces.

Tehran is seeking a hasty retreat by the United States and its partners that will leave a political and security vacuum that Iran can readily fill, dragging Iraq into its sphere of influence—or, perhaps, carving off southern Iraq to create an Iranian "super state."

Without question, Iranian encroachment on Iraq must be prevented at all costs.

Iran's Motives in Iraq

Some Middle East experts don't buy this take on Iran's involvement in Iraq, especially its geopolitical intentions. Yet Tehran plainly has every reason to want to see the U.S.-led Coalition in Iraq fail.

First, since the 1979 revolution, the "Great Satan" [America] has been Iran's No. 1 enemy. The radical regime found it bad enough having American forces in the region before the Afghan and Iraqi wars, much less having 150,000 cranky, battle-hardened GIs right next door.

Now, Tehran faces not only the prospects of (at least some) American forces being stationed long-term in the theater, a fundamental check on Iranian power, but also the possibility that Iraq and Afghanistan could become strong U.S. allies.

Second, Iran's rulers are deathly afraid that the freedoms taking root in Iraq/Afghanistan will highlight the Iranian revolution's abject political, economic and social failures to Iran's increasingly discontented "baby-boomers." Iran's people (60 percent are under the age of 30, born after the revolution) will look more and more at the political, economic and social freedoms enjoyed by Iraqis and Afghans and ask: "Why not us?"

Third, Iran is a Shia Persian country in a tough Sunni Arab neighborhood. Bringing southern Shia-majority Iraq under Iranian influence—or, even, via secession from Iraq or civil war, Iranian control—will neuter long-time enemy Iraq as a threat.

Absorbing southern Iraq would not only debilitate Baghdad by cutting off access to Persian Gulf seaports, it would significantly increase Iran's size, population and oil wealth, putting Tehran on a trajectory to regional dominance.

It is true that weapons, clearly, unambiguously, from Iran have been found in Iraq.

Iran's Tactics in Iraq

Iran has been slipping clerics, intelligence agents and paramilitary forces into Iraq and bankrolling sympathizers, political parties and militants since the spring 2003 [U.S.] invasion to bring Iraq under its sway—while doing its best to keep its fingerprints off its dirty dealings.

But seeing Coalition forces facing a tough insurgency, Iran evidently decided to seize the opportunity to advance its cause, upping the ante by changing its tactics from garnering influence to actively instigating insurgency against U.S.-Coalition forces—even Iraqis who might stand in the way.

You want proof? Well, Coalition forces recently intercepted a number of shipments of explosives being spirited across the border from Iran to Iraq. Experts believe that a new, more lethal-type of roadside bomb—capable of destroying armored vehicles—is based on an Iranian design often used in the past by Hezbollah against Israel.

[In August 2005], Defense Secretary Donald Rumsfeld, seemingly choking off a desire to be more direct, said: "It is true that weapons, clearly, unambiguously, from Iran have been found in Iraq." Another senior officer claimed that the new bombs are, "the most sophisticated and most lethal devices we've seen."

But it's more than just these new deadly explosives: The Iranian Revolutionary Guard Corps–directed component of the insurgency probably consists of several hundred Iranians and Iraqis as well as members of Lebanon's Iranian-backed, Shia terrorist group, Hezbollah.

Some analysts believe the Iranian paramilitaries and Iranian-supported militias are training insurgents in southern Iraq as well as in Iran. In addition, it's likely that Iranian-led insurgents are being prepped by Hezbollah guerrillas in southern Lebanon and the Bekaa Valley.

The American Reaction

Iranian behavior is increasingly troubling and problematic for U.S. national security and regional interests—an Iranian-directed insurgency in Iraq is just the latest example of Persian perfidy.

It's time to stop handling Iran with kid gloves, especially while Iranian hi-tech bombs deployed by Tehran-backed insurgents are killing Coalition and Iraqi forces and civilians, encouraging civil war and destabilizing the country.

It's time for an aggressive rollback strategy against the Iranian regime—to address its drive for nuclear weapons, its sponsorship of terror is Iraq and elsewhere, and its repressive rule at home. The strategy should embrace biting economic sanctions, aggressive covert action—and even surgical military strikes to protect American and Coalition forces and interests.

7

Iran's Interventions in Iraq Have Been More Helpful than Harmful

Kenneth M. Pollack

Kenneth M. Pollack is a Senior Fellow in Foreign Policy at the Brookings Institution, a Washington, D.C., research institute, and a former member of the National Security Council. He is the author of several books, including The Persian Puzzle: The Conflict Between Iran and America.

Iran has a considerable capacity to make life in Iraq difficult for the American military, but it has no reason to do so. Unrest from a chaotic Iraq would be likely to spill over into Iran, which is not in the interest of the Iranian government. Moreover, a stable, democratic Iraq is likely to be led by a Shia-dominated government that would presumably be friendly to Shia-majority Iran even without Iranian intervention. The Iranian government's actions support this view; although the Iranian intelligence services are present in Iraq, they have with only a few exceptions avoided attacking Americans or the Iraqi government. As long as Iran has no reason to fear that the United States is trying to set up an anti-Iranian puppet government in Baghdad, its general noninterference will presumably continue.

Kenneth M. Pollack, statement before the U.S. House Armed Services Committee, Washington, D.C., September 29, 2005.

[A] potential menace to American interests is the possibility that at some point, Iran might choose to actively fight the American reconstruction efforts in Iraq. Because of the extent of Iranian influence and presence in Iraq, this could have devastating consequences. . . . America's challenges in Iraq are great enough with Iran being mostly supportive of our efforts; if Iran were to turn against us, those problems would increase dramatically—perhaps even insurmountably. Of course, Iraq (and Afghanistan) are two-way streets: Iran needs the United States to stabilize those countries to prevent them from sliding into chaos, so Iran has every incentive to continue to be supportive of American efforts, as long as those efforts are aimed at building a stable, pluralist, and independent Iraq.

During Operation Iraqi Freedom in March–April 2003, Iran was not as helpful as it had been in the Afghan war, but it certainly was not unhelpful. The IRGC [Islamic Revolutionary Guard Corps] seems to have been put on its best behavior and did not create any problems for the U.S.-led Coalition. After the war, Iran proved to be of considerable assistance to the American reconstruction effort, arguably more helpful than it had been in Afghanistan. Tehran did not do so out of the goodness of its heart. The Iranian leadership, which understood Iraqi society far better than much of the [George W.] Bush Administration, recognized early on that stabilizing Iraq after the fall of Saddam [Hussein]'s totalitarian dictatorship, and then building a functional pluralistic political system afterwards, were going to be herculean tasks. They were also precisely what Tehran wanted to see happen in Iraq, because they believed this would ensure that Iraq did not slide into civil war and chaos (which was Iran's greatest fear and first priority) and because doing so would mean a Shi'ah-dominated government which might not be Iran's proxy, but was unlikely to be hostile to it either. Given that the Iranians seem to have had rather low expectations for postwar Iraq, just achieving those goals were enough for them. That said, there is no question that Iran has actively aided those Iraqis whom they believe will be most likely to want good relations with Iran, and might even prove subservient to Tehran. However, it has done so within the context of largely fostering the same kind of political process that the United States has sought.

Consequently, Tehran told its various proxy groups in Iraq not to resist the United States and instead to participate in the U.S.-led process of reconstruction. This was critical because many of the most important Shi'ah groups, such as ad-Dawa and the Supreme Council for the Islamic Revolution in Iraq (SCIRI), as well as key individuals like famed guerrilla commander 'Abd al-Karim Mahud al-Muhammadawi, had all been supported by Iran in one fashion or another during the 1980s and '90s. In addition, many other Iraqi Shi'ah would likely have looked to Iran as their natural protector in the event of a fight for supremacy. Iran's quiet encouragement of all of these groups was critical to their early participation in the U.S.-led process of political and economic reconstruction, and their willingness to stay the course when initial American mistakes created tremendous problems with lawlessness, economic chaos, and the threat of a political collapse, was critical in keeping the situation from spiraling out of control. If the Iranians had wanted to cause chaos in Iraq, they could have easily done so in the darkest days after the war, and the United States was fortunate that they did not.

The Iranian Presence in Iraq

Of course, since it was Iran, it was not as simple as just that. Soon after the end of major combat operations in May 2003, American officials in Iraq began to detect the first Iranian intelligence personnel moving into the country. Over time, this flow began to increase. By early 2004, all of Iran's various intelligence and covert action organizations were represented in Iraq—the IRGC (including its Quds Forces), Hizballah, the MOIS [Ministry of Intelligence and Security], Lebanese Hizballah, and assorted others. Their mere presence in Iraq has been alarming, but American officials and intelligence officers in Iraq have stressed a critical fact: the Iranians were in Iraq in strength, and were building a very large intelligence network, but that network was not "operational." In the parlance of the American military, it has not "gone kinetic." In other words, it was not attempting to attack the United States, and instead has concentrated on gathering information and strengthening itself. Reports have surfaced of Iranian-backed assassinations of key Sunni figures and even some of assistance to some of the Sunni groups within the insurgency. However, even if true, and it seems likely that a number of these reports were accurate, they still constitute rather minor activities on Iran's part. In the semi-chaos of post-Saddam Iraq, there have been numerous opportunities for the Iranians to attack (or even surveil) Americans, encourage one Iraqi group to attack another, terrorize populations into acquiescing to their wishes, or otherwise add to the violence—both political and random—in the country. But so far they have largely avoided doing so.

Indeed, the only time that American or Iraqi officials were able to demonstrate an Iranian "action" inside Iraq came in February 2004, when a group of Iranians was arrested by the Iraqi police in Sunni-controlled Fallujah. The next week, the Iranians staged an attack on the police station that allowed their comrades to escape. Four attackers were killed in the assault, and their papers indicated that one was an Iranian and two others were Lebanese. It is worth noting that this attack was far more skillful than what Coalition forces had seen from the Iraqis themselves. "The attack on the police was unusually bold and sophisticated," the New York Times reported based on the accounts of American military officers, "with the insurgents advancing from four sides, firing heavy machine guns and rocket-propelled grenades. The assault on the police station was coupled with a simultaneous attack on an Iraqi civil defense headquarters about a mile away, intended to hold them in check while the prison break unfolded. In all, the insurgents numbered 30 to 50, operating with heavy firepower in daylight." This single event underscores the point that had the Iranians wanted to cause trouble for the U.S.-led reconstruction of Iraq, they could have made the situation infinitely worse than it already was.

Given that Iran's . . . populace has been growing ever more unhappy with its economic plight, Tehran does not need any more instability imported from a chaotic Iraq.

Iran's Internal Foreign Policy Debate

Iran's seemingly inexplicable behavior in Iraq makes considerable sense when viewed as part of the ongoing battles over foreign policy within Iran. Naturally, the reformists pushed for cooperation with the United States, but by 2003–2004 their wishes counted for little in foreign policy debates in Tehran. Then-President [Mohammed] Khatami mostly mimicked whatever [Ayatollah Ali] Khamene'i said on an issue, although perhaps without quite the Supreme Leader's conviction. Instead, the critical debate seems to have been between the most extreme elements among the Iranian hard-liners—the Pasdaran [another name for the IRGC] some members of the Council of Guardians, influential Majles [parliament] members, and others—on the one hand, and the mainstream Iranian leadership concentrated in Khamene'i, [former president Akbar Hashemi] Rafsanjani, and some emerging figures such as the Secretary General of Iran's Supreme National Security Council, Hasan Ruhani, on the other. It was the principal leadership that apparently concluded that Iran's interests would be best served by seeing the American plan to build a stable, pluralist, and independent Iraq succeed. With over 130,000 American troops in Iraq, they did not want to provoke an American military operation against Iran. Moreover, their greatest fear has been that the U.S.-led occupation would fail, pushing Iraq into chaos, which they believed would likely spill over into Iran. Given that Iran's economy continues to flounder even with $60+ per barrel oil prices and its populace has been growing ever more unhappy with its economic plight, Tehran does not need any more instability imported from a chaotic Iraq. Consequently, Iran's mainstream leadership seems to have seen no reason to try to oppose the Americans and every reason to support the U.S., albeit at arm's length.

Typically, many of the firebrands in Tehran seem to have had a different view of the situation. They appear to have argued for moving into Iraq in force and using everything at their disposal—money, supplies, promises, threats, assassinations, and large-scale violence—either to secure power for one or more groups loyal to themselves, or to build up proxies and drive out Sunni Arabs and Kurds from southern and eastern Iraq to create buffers and protectorates within the country. We do not know their logic, but one of two intertwined reasons seems most likely. Many in Iran feared that the United States intended to create a pro-American puppet regime in Baghdad, one that might even serve as the launch-pad for an invasion of Iran in the near future. It seems likely that the Iranian extremists shared this view and so may have argued that Iran should get into Iraq and start fighting to undermine the Americans right away to prevent this from happening. Alternatively, it may be that the Iranian extremists simply did not believe that Washington could achieve its goal of creating a stable, pluralistic Iraq. This was a view held by many people throughout the region. In this case, the extremists likely would have maintained that since the United States was bound to fail, it was critical for Iran to put itself in a position to be able to guard its own interests when the

Americans did fail, which likely would plunge the country into chaos and civil war. In this defensive version of the scenario, the extremists would have been arguing that it was only prudent for Iran to take prophylactic measures to prevent a worst-case scenario in the future.

Khamene'i, always overly indulgent of his far right because of his insecurity about his legitimacy as *faqih* [chief jurist], appears to have agreed to a compromise. He seems to have allowed the intelligence services to deploy to Iraq in force and position themselves to fight a war there if necessary, but not to engage in belligerent activities until ordered to do so. So the Iranians have been recruiting assets; reconnoitering the terrain; securing allies, distributing weapons, money and supplies; establishing safe houses and other facilities; setting up a logistical and communications network; training their personnel; and even drawing up operational plans, but they do not appear to have been authorized to take action against the Americans and have been limited in the actions they have taken against other Iraqi groups.

Iran has so far been more helpful in advancing the causes of stability and democracy in Iraq than it has been hurtful.

Iran's "Plan B"

In this sense, Iran's activities in Iraq are not only designed to help their friends attain power in the nascent Iraqi government, but also serves as Tehran's "Plan B." If at some point Tehran decides either that the Americans are attempting to create a puppet government in Iraq (especially one meant to serve as a launching pad for an invasion of Iran) or that the U.S.-led reconstruction effort is going to fail, likely creating the chaos that is Iran's worst nightmare, then Tehran would unleash the Iranian intelligence services to protect Iranian interests as best they could. (And they had learned a tremendous amount from their experience in a similar environment in Lebanon in the 1980s and '90s). Since the intelligence services have already done much of the preparatory work necessary to build a base for such operations, Iran will be well-placed to defend its interests in that scenario as well.

Iran's activities in Iraq are not intended to benefit the United States and some have been downright harmful. They have provided some degree of assistance to Muqtada al-Sadr and other Shi'ah rejectionists. They have probably helped assassinate some Sunni leaders, some of whom might have proven to be able advocates for that community, and any such killings can only escalate the risk of civil war. They have otherwise helped Iraqi leaders with close ties to Tehran who may not prove to be friends of the United States. However, we should be careful not to exaggerate the extent of Iran's nefarious activities in Iraq. For many Iraqis and many Americans, it is easy to blame our problems in Iraq on Iran, much easier than to confront the hard truth that most of those problems are of our own making and so cannot be solved by simply beating the Iranian bugbear. Moreover, we also need to consider carefully the very important tacit cooperation we have had from the Iranians in advancing the general course of reconstruction in Iraq. Although we may not necessarily like all of the same people in Iraq, on balance, Iran has so far been more helpful in advancing the causes of stability and democracy in Iraq than it has been hurtful.

8

Diplomacy Is the Best Option for American-Iranian Relations

Stephen Kinzer

Stephen Kinzer is a journalist and author. His books include All the Shah's Men: An American Coup and the Roots of Middle East Terror *and* Overthrow: America's Century of Regime Change from Hawaii to Iraq.

Iran is not the monolithically conservative country that many Westerners believe it to be. Many of its citizens are disillusioned with the conservative regime, and even within the government a large number of officials are believers in reform and democracy. Even Iranians who oppose their present regime, however, do not want to see the United States impose political change on their country. Under these circumstances, America's best course of action is to engage with the Iranian government and people, attempt to improve the relationship between the two countries, and allow the reformers within the country to bring about change at their own pace.

Stephen Kinzer, "Handle with Care: Iraq We've Invaded. North Korea We Won't. That Leaves Iran, Where Most People Are Eager for Change—But Not the Kind That Current U.S. Policy Would Deliver. Here's a Smarter Way," *American Prospect*, vol. 15, April 2004, p. 37. Copyright 2004 The American Prospect, Inc. All rights reserved. Reproduced with permission from The American Prospect, 11 Beacon Street, Suite 1120, Boston, MA 02108.

"You did a great thing!"

With that unexpected greeting from an Iranian diplomat in New York [in] December [2003], my trip to Iran began to take shape. A few months earlier I had published a book that tells how, in 1953, the CIA [Central Intelligence Agency] deposed Iran's last democratic leader, Mohammed Mossadegh, and set his country on a path toward dictatorship and tragedy. Because my book honors Mossadegh, who was a secular liberal and who detested fundamentalism, I hardly expected any representative of the current Iranian regime, especially one who would rule on my visa application, to praise it.

I soon realized, however, that this government official is one of the many Iranians dedicated to the ideals of reform and reconciliation with the West, especially the United States. Most Iranians I had spoken with on previous visits share these views. They are frustrated by their lack of freedom and their country's isolation in the world. In whatever ways they can, they are pressing for social and political change.

A couple of years earlier, while in the process of researching my book, I had had enormous trouble getting into Iran. Now, suddenly, everything seemed to have changed. The difference could only be that I had published my book resurrecting the figure of Mossadegh. Iran does not observe international copyright conventions, and my book was quickly pirated, translated into Persian, and put on sale in Iran. Readers, especially Iranian readers, might take it as a story of how much Iran was poised to achieve under democratic rule—and how much it lost by falling under royal and then religious tyranny. For better or worse, I became associated with Mossadegh's view that democracy is the best form of government for Iran. Today's Iranian reformers also believe that, and their enthusiasm undoubtedly was behind the warm praise with which this Iranian diplomat received my visa application at the end of 2003.

Iran, however, has two governments. One is a functioning democracy, complete with elections, a feisty press, and a cadre of reformist politicians. The other is a narrow-minded clique of mullahs that has lost touch with the masses and sometimes seems to have no agenda other than closing newspapers and blocking democratic change. These governments vie for power every day. Outsiders may be forgiven for seeing Iran as a country that can never make up its mind. Should it punish the prison guards who beat a photographer to death [in 2003], or promote them? Should it cooperate with foreigners who want to monitor its nuclear program, or defy them? Should it allow reformers to run for parliament, or ban them? Iranian officials seem to contradict themselves endlessly on these and countless other questions, changing their positions from one day to the next. Behind that apparent indecision is a constant struggle between the old guard and the democratic insurgents. One group is dominant for a while, then the other surges back.

As the time for my January [2004] trip to Iran approached, I began contacting people there to arrange interviews. Among them were powerful figures in the religious regime, some of whom seemed alarmed to learn that a journalist who had written favorably about Mossadegh was being allowed into the country. A few hours before I was to leave, I received a startling message from the Iranian diplomatic mission in New York: Stay home or risk arrest at the Tehran airport.

I will probably never know what led to this sudden change in the regime's attitude toward me, but I have a theory: Probably I was caught in the same power struggle that envelops all of Iranian public life. Those who promoted my trip and obtained my visa so quickly did so because they hoped I would help propagate their ideals in Iran. Their conservative rivals also suspected I would do that, and when they learned I was coming, they stepped in to cancel my trip.

Iran's Ideological Divisions

What happened in Iran at the beginning of [2004], when I was supposed to be there, reflected the same ideological tug-of-war that made Iranian officials unable to decide on such a small matter as my visa. A full-fledged political crisis erupted as the parliament, which represents Iranian democracy, clashed with the shadowy Council of Guardians, the voice of reaction and fundamentalism. The council issued an order disqualifying nearly half of the 8,200 candidates who wished to run for seats in parliament. Among them were more than 80 of the 290 incumbents, including no less symbolic a figure than President Mohammed Khatami's brother. That order triggered a 26-day protest sit-in, a round of recriminations, and, in the end, an election that turned out badly for everyone. Reformers lost most of their seats, including that of Speaker Mehdi Karoubi. Conservatives lost much of what little democratic credibility they had left. But the clearest losers of all were the Iranian people. For now, at least, the option of change through the ballot box is closed to them.

In response to the crisis, Khatami issued statements questioning the Council of Guardians, but refused to challenge it or to criticize Ayatollah Ali Khamenei, the country's unelected "supreme leader." That has been a huge disappointment to voters, who elected Khatami in a landslide in 1997 and then again in 2001. Unable or unwilling to fulfill the nation's reformist hopes, he has gone from the role of national savior to the butt of crude jokes. One of them tells of a woman who has been married for years but is still a virgin. When asked how this is possible, she replies: "My husband is President Khatami. He keeps saying 'I'll do it, I'll do it,' but he never does it."

Because politicians have been so unsuccessful in challenging the clerical regime, many Iranians have lost faith not only in them but in the entire political process. Deprived of the chance to vote for candidates of their choice, they stay away from the polls in droves. Their frustration is quite different from the fatalistic lassitude that has shrouded much of the rest of the Middle East for centuries. Iranians are a highly cultured, educated people with a rich history who trace their lineage to the Persian Emperor Cyrus, author of what is sometimes described as history's first human-rights declaration. (Shirin Ebadi, the Iranian lawyer who won the 2003 Nobel Peace Prize, introduced herself in Oslo as "a descendent of Cyrus the Great, the very emperor who proclaimed at the pinnacle of power 2,500 years ago that he 'would not reign over the people if they did not wish it.'")

For more than a century, Iranians have painstakingly been making their way toward democracy. Iran has the human and natural resources to be at least as successful as regional powers like Mexico, Turkey, and Malaysia, but its people suffer under a regime whose failures have given them both an undemocratic political system and plagues of unemployment, corruption, drug abuse, child prostitution, and other forms of social decay. Many find escape in a burgeoning subculture that revolves around the Internet, satellite television, and other subversive tools, but they shy away from political action because no cause or leader captures their imagination.

[2004]'s confrontation over who should be allowed to run for parliament was widely covered in the Western press. Some officials in Washington eagerly interpreted it as a sign of the regime's impending collapse. In Iran, however, it was no big deal. Friends of mine there, whom I heard from by e-mail after my trip was canceled, were unanimous in their disgust.

"The sit-in sounds more serious outside the country," a journalist wrote. "Most people see it as a political show by reformers to attract people's support. I highly doubt that they would have been able to get elected even if they were allowed to run. Many say that they were cheated when they voted for the reformers, and that reformers are deeply faithful to the system." A student in his mid-20s was just as pessimistic. "The reformers have missed golden opportunities since the presidential election in 1997," he lamented. "Now they want to compensate, but it is so late. People ignore them. We know the conservatives are the worst alternative, but the reformists are a bad one. We are looking for new faces, but there is no one."

Iranians fervently wish for change, but not through revolution.

No Revolution, No Regime Change

If so many people in Iran are so unhappy with their government, why don't they rise up and overthrow it? During my last visit there, [in late 2002], I put this question to various people. All gave me the same answer. One university professor put it most succinctly. "We all banded together to overthrow the shah in 1979, everyone from communists to Mossadegh liberals to religious fanatics," he told me. "We were able to work together because we all agreed on one thing: Nothing could be worse than the shah. But what happened? We got something worse. We learned a terrible lesson. You don't want to go out onto the streets and start the wheel of revolution rolling. You never know where it will lead. It's better to be patient and unhappy than risk another catastrophe."

Iranians fervently wish for change, but not through revolution. Nor, despite the fantasies of some in Washington, would they welcome foreign intervention. Such intervention, in fact, would probably be the only thing that would bring many of them to support the regime they loathe. After all, the country's bitter history has led many Iranians to consider foreign intervention the greatest evil that could befall them. The British robbed them of their oil wealth during the first half of the 20th century, British and American agents organized the coup that crushed their democracy in 1953, and Americans propped up Shah Mohammed Reza Pahlavi for 25 years.

Early in the Bush administration, some policy planners seriously considered the possibility of sending troops to overthrow the Iranian government. "Everyone wants to go to Baghdad. Real men want to go to Tehran," a British official working with the Bush team said ominously in mid-2002. If the American soldiers who invaded Iraq had been greeted with garlands of flowers instead of guerrilla resistance, those "real men" might well have sent them on. Some militants still argue for it. David Frum and Richard Perle, now that they have cut their official ties with the White House and are free to express views that their friends in the Bush administration may still hold, assert in their new book *An End to Evil* that the Iranian regime "must go." . . . They urge the United States to crush it "with no more compunction than a police sharpshooter feels when he downs a hostage-taker."

Public opinion in Iran is strongly in favor of democratic reform, and that reform will come, albeit not nearly as quickly as most Americans would like.

History warns against that course. The U.S.-sponsored coup of 1953 led to decades of upheaval in Iran. It turned the country toward tyranny and led to the rise of a regime that has used every tactic at its disposal, including terrorism, to undermine American interests in the world. Public opinion in Iran is strongly in favor of democratic reform, and that reform will come, albeit not nearly as quickly as most Americans would like. Intervention would not only turn a new generation against the United States but also end Iran's fitful progress back toward the democracy it lost after the CIA coup of 1953.

Better Diplomatic Relations?

There will not be any invasion of Iran [in 2004]. Nor, unfortunately, is there likely to be any advance in Iranian-American relations. Part of the reason is that foreign policy circles in Washington and Tehran mirror one another. One group in each capital favors reconciliation, and they have been in sporadic contact with each other over the years, including during the Bush administration. Their efforts, however, are repeatedly sabotaged by hard-liners in both capitals, who have spent years in confrontation mode.

Iran is not a closed garrison state like North Korea, and its clerical regime is not a self-destructive dictatorship like Saddam Hussein's. Its leaders, including the dour mullahs, are eminently rational, and they now appear more willing to listen to proposals from Washington than at any time since they seized power in 1979. Despite President Khatami's evident failures, he has shifted the center of political gravity in Iran. Political and social ideas are more freely debated there now than at any time in half a century. Women must still wear veils, but vigilantes no longer brutalize those who show their hair, wear makeup, or talk to men in public. [In 2004], for the first time in 25 years, British artists will show their work at a Tehran museum and American archeologists will work at sites in the Iranian desert. The government has invited members of the U.S. Congress to visit.

Engagement is the best tool the West has to encourage change in Iran.

The Bush administration has been unable to decide how to respond to these overtures. Some officials apparently believe that the United States should not engage with Iran simply because it makes no sense to negotiate with a regime one wishes to destroy (or at least hopes will soon collapse). That is foolish, as engagement is the best tool the West has to encourage change in Iran. There are, however, several good reasons for caution.

Reasons for Caution

Officials in Washington are rightly concerned about Iran's nuclear aspirations, and rightly dubious that Iran will keep its promise not to produce nuclear weapons. Seen from the Iranian perspective, the nuclear project makes perfect sense. Israel, the only country in the region that is truly Iran's enemy, has nuclear weapons. So does the United States, which has troops on both Iran's western border (in Iraq) and its eastern border (in Afghanistan), and whose president has famously designated Iran as part of the world's "axis of evil." One certain way for Iran to deter an attack from either of these hostile powers would be to do what India, Pakistan, and North Korea have done: develop nuclear weapons. Only if the United States stops threatening Iran, and instead accepts some arrangement that offers it a place in a new Middle Eastern security structure, can it be seriously expected to curb its nuclear ambitions.

The administration is also put off by Iran's atrocious record of sponsoring terrorism around the world. Iranian agents, acting with the support of at least some factions in the regime, have assassinated dissident exiles in various European capitals, launched attacks on American military bases, and even, according to several intelligence agencies, planned the 1994 bombing of a Jewish community center in Buenos Aires, Argentina, that took 85 lives. The regime may have pulled back from this murderous course of late, but it must offer credible assurances to that effect if it expects serious dialogue with Washington. It still supports groups that militantly oppose the current Middle East peace process, yet even that seems open to negotiation. Khatami recently asserted that if Palestinians were offered a deal they wished to accept, Iran would not "impose [its] views on others or stand in their way." Resolving the Israeli-Palestinian dispute is an absolute prerequisite to stability in the Middle East, and although Iran has been no friend of the peace process, its very militancy could make it a uniquely valuable force if it could be enticed to moderate its position.

Many leading Democrats agree that engagement with Iran would bring better results than confrontation but are afraid of being labeled as softies. . . .

The overwhelming majority of Iranians want peaceful change; the United States should embrace their cause.

So [do] some influential Republicans. "Engagement is the right policy, even though it's very difficult to do at times," Senator Richard Shelby, former chairman of the Senate Intelligence Committee, told me recently. "Military confrontation would be wrong unless it's forced on us, because the Iranians would all rally to their government. We should be looking for ways to do business with them, and then wait for the profound changes that I think are coming."

A Sensible Iran Policy

What would make a sensible U.S. policy toward Iran? First, the United States should accept the reality of the Islamic revolution and commit itself to a peaceful resolution of differences between the two countries. Iran is in a period of transition, and it is in everyone's interest to allow this process to proceed. The overwhelming majority of Iranians want peaceful change; the United States should embrace their cause.

Second, in approaching Iran, American officials should bear in mind that this is a country where rhetoric is unusually important. For a combination of historical, cultural, and religious reasons, Iranians feel a deep-seated need to be approached respectfully. American leaders can and should make clear that their interest is in reaching out to help the Iranian people, not the ruling clerics. If they take an accusing or commanding or imperious tone, however, they cannot expect a good response.

Third, the United States should recognize that change in Iran will have to come from within. Iranians will reject any faction that Washington endorses, especially if it is based outside the country. For more than a century, resistance to foreign intervention has shaped Iranian politics. It is folly to believe that Iranians are any more likely to accept intervention now than they were in the past.

Restraint, engagement, and the support of allies brought about America's epochal victory in the Cold War. The same formula can work today in Iran.

Finally, American leaders should approach Iran together with allies, especially the European Union. One of the few recent successes the Iranian regime can claim has been the repairing of its ties with Europe. Iranian leaders know that they must strengthen those ties if they are to improve their economy and emerge from political isolation. European officials brokered [2003]'s deal between Iran and the International Atomic Energy Agency, and Iran will be especially eager to begin talks with the United States if Europeans are also involved.

To embark on this policy, the United States would have to recognize that Iran is not in a revolutionary or prerevolutionary state, that it is essentially stable despite the continual bickering among political factions, and that its people do not wish for either revolution or foreign intervention. Some powerful figures in the Bush administration, captured by messianic visions and convinced that American power can achieve any goal, refuse to accept these facts and want the United States to intervene in Iran. Only by resisting that temptation can the United States hope to reach a grand bargain that would integrate Iran into a peaceful Middle East. Such a bargain is now at least conceivable. American leaders should pursue it seriously, because detente between Tehran and Washington could help reshape the world's most volatile region.

Restraint, engagement, and the support of allies brought about America's epochal victory in the Cold War. The same formula can work today in Iran.

9

Diplomacy Is Not an Effective Option for Dealing with Iran

Reuel Marc Gerecht

Reuel Marc Gerecht is a senior fellow at the American Enterprise Institute and a former Middle East expert for the Central Intelligence Agency. His books include Know Thine Enemy: A Spy's Journey into Revolutionary Iran *and* The Islamic Paradox: Shiite Clerics, Sunni Fundamentalists, and the Coming of Arab Democracy.

The United States and the European Union will not succeed in using diplomacy to prevent Iran from getting nuclear weapons. The long-running European-led negotiations with Iran over its nuclear program have gone nowhere, and the United States and European Union have few diplomatic options left. Imposing sanctions on Iran would drive the price of oil higher, which is unacceptable to the West, and the United States is not prepared to give financial incentives to a country with Iran's record of supporting international terrorism. Internal unrest in Iran may lead to a less militant government taking power there, but the United States is not in a position to control this process. The threat of military force is the only remaining, plausible option the United States has for preventing Iran from developing nuclear weapons.

Reuel Marc Gerecht, "Bush's Great Middle East Gamble: The Best Hope for Iran Is Winning in Iraq," *Weekly Standard*, vol. 11, November 14, 2005, p. 29. Copyright © 2005, News Corporation, Weekly Standard. All rights reserved. Reproduced by permission.

Iraq may actually be a bright spot in the [George W.] Bush administration's foreign policy, compared with Iran. With Iraq, a hard-nosed, historically sensitive person can have considerable, well-founded hope. With clerical Iran—still the greater nightmare for the United States—it's difficult to sustain any optimism. A knowledgeable observer would have to conclude that the clerical regime—which, properly understood, is a somewhat more conservative, cautious variation on the Sunni holy warriorism that struck us on 9/11—is going to get the Bomb despite the Bush administration's limited efforts to stop it. And again, contrary to the accepted wisdom in Washington, restraint in responding to clerical Iran's quest for nuclear weapons is much more likely to cause problems in Iraq than a muscular approach to countering Tehran's ambitions.

In Iranian eyes, the American-backed European Union's nuclear negotiations with the mullahs are not serious enough to be frightening. The EU-3—the British, the Germans, and the French—have in their own words gone as far as they can go in their soft-power negotiations with Iran's ruling clergy. The resurgence of Iran's hottest revolutionary sentiments under President [Mahmoud] Ahmadinejad and the recall of prominent "moderate" Iranian ambassadors from Europe is unlikely to change Europe's philosophy and tactics for dealing with the Iranian nuclear problem. The EU-3—at least for certain the French and the Germans—want Washington to introduce massive incentives—the dictionary definition of this is "appeasement" —to continue the West's "dialogue" with the mullahs.

The administration's response, understandably, has so far been silence. But continuous quiet reflection is not a policy, even when the CIA's analysts self-defensively throw up their hands and announce that they have no idea when Tehran is going to get nuclear weapons. (Unless Langley [CIA Headquarters] gets lucky with an Iranian "walk-in" who volunteers detailed, critical information about Tehran's weapons program, the CIA will probably only know the mullahs have the Bomb after they detonate it.) It is easy to appreciate the administration's predicament with the Islamic Republic: Counterproliferation does not lend itself to soft power. But the State Department, with Undersecretary of State Nicholas Burns in the lead, now controls Iran policy. The decision by the administration to embrace the EU-3 negotiations was an interesting experiment in post-Iraq war transatlantic relations: We would let the Europeans de facto own our Iran policy. By giving them this responsibility, so the appealing theory goes, we would encourage their maturity and their greater willingness to implement severe sanctions against the Islamic Republic if it didn't relent in developing its nuclear energy/weapons program. (To the EU-3's credit, it's very hard to find a participant in this affair who actually believes the Iranians aren't trying to develop nuclear weapons.)

It is impossible to overstate the U.S. government's— particularly the CIA's—unpreparedness to start finding, encouraging, and materially backing the internal Iranian opposition to the ruling clergy.

The theory hasn't worked, of course. And it's pretty hard to blame the Europeans since they've been forthright from the beginning: They have never said they would be willing to impose tough sanctions on Iran for its nuclear misbehavior. The Europeans are also quick to point out, quite correctly, that the Americans have never really discussed sanctions either, since both sides know any biting sanction would touch Iran's oil industry. Sanctioning the Islamic Republic with the price of oil at $60 a barrel would require a certain fortitude, which neither side has (the Europeans, again, are at least honest in saying this). Secretary of State Condoleezza Rice is obviously fearful of taking Iran to the United Nations Security Council since we will surely lose a vote there. Russia and China will not cooperate. The Germans might not, either. The idea of creating another sanctions regime confined to the G-7 industrial nations—an idea now circulating in Washington—is also a pipe dream since the Europeans have already made it crystal clear that they won't even embargo automobile parts to the Islamic Republic, let alone anything that might bring greater and more immediate pain.

The Bush administration has quite understandably allowed this game to go on. The policy alternatives are onerous: preventively bomb the nuclear-related facilities and implement an aggressive containment and pro-democracy strategy, or implement the difficult containment/democracy strategy without bombing the nuclear facilities. It is impossible to overstate the U.S. government's—particularly the CIA's—unpreparedness to start finding, encouraging, and materially backing the internal Iranian opposition to the ruling clergy. No doubt the Bush administration would like to punt the problem back into European hands. The Europeans don't want it, however, unless the United States gives them more goodies to dangle in front of the revolutionary clergy's eyes. (E.U. diplomacy naturally assumes that everyone is, or ought to be, avariciously pragmatic.)

Washington isn't going to do this, even if the clerical regime decides again, as it appears to be doing, to suggest some flexibility in its negotiating positions. (Opening up the Parchin military facility to inspections would be an example of a not particularly meaningful "softening" in the regime's position.) Some in the administration, especially in the Near East Bureau of the State Department, may want to try more incentives. The Iran policy paper recently leaked to the *Wall Street Journal* certainly shows a desire, strongest in the Department of State, to appease Iran further since the alternatives are convulsive. But the culture, politics, and history of the clerical regime in Tehran make this a difficult sell.

Just imagine an American diplomat actually promising security guarantees to an Iranian counterpart: "We hereby promise to leave Afghanistan and Iraq—installing in each a government to your liking—and to quit Central Asia. And we double promise never ever to talk about democracy in Iran again, and no more personal insults to the Spiritual Leader Ali Khamenei, which we know you find very offensive." Then imagine the same scenario with generous financial goodies attached up front, as the clerics would certainly demand. It is difficult to conceive of even a President John Kerry or a President Hillary Clinton handing over billions of dollars to clerics and Revolutionary Guardsmen, like the current Iranian president Mahmoud Ahmadinejad, who have a long record of supporting anti-American terrorism, not to mention other nefarious causes. In a pre-9/11 world, when so-called moderate Iranian clerics were our interlocutors, this didn't seem culturally, intellectually, politically, or strategically plausible. Now, it just seems surreal.

The only way Iran is going to get better is for it to get a lot worse—and Ahmadinejad may just possibly be the man to galvanize a broad-based opposition to the regime.

Ahmadinejad, who is an unvarnished revolutionary, makes even the Europeans blanch (they still won't support sanctions, but they do blanch). The Iranian president's recently expressed desire to wipe Israel off the map was a vivid reminder that Iran's ruling elite are still, on the important issues, faithful children of Ayatollah Ruhollah Khomeini. Ahmadinejad is, of course, fundamentally no different from former President Mohammad Khatami, who loathed Israel as only a very left-wing cleric can, or Iran's leader, Ali Khamenei, who often gives the impression that he's memorized every single line of the Persian edition of the anti-Semitic Protocols of the Elders of Zion, or Ali Akbar Hashemi Rafsanjani, who is in the West probably the most misunderstood cleric in the Islamic Republic. For the Europeans, and some in the Bush administration, Rafsanjani was the white-turbaned hope, the real politician-pragmatist who would save the West from a showdown over Iran's nuclear-weapons program. In reality, he is the true father of Iran's nuclear-bomb program, an overlord for the Iranian terrorism that struck Europe in the 1980s and '90s, and quite possibly one of the dark princes behind the domestic assassination campaign of Iranian liberals that began in the late 1990s. Concerning Israel, Rafsanjani has never given any indication that he differs with the Palestinian Islamic Jihad, a group Rafsanjani has always supported: Israelis are best when dead.

Which brings us back to where we were [in 2003]: Are we willing to use military force to back up a nuclear counterproliferation regime against a state with a long record in terrorism, whose ruling elite is probably the most anti-American on earth? If we are not, then nuclear counterproliferation is effectively over. Iran's ruling clergy has enormous tenacity and a sixth sense for weakness (that's how they downed the shah). Unfortunately, the EU-3 negotiations have left us looking increasingly weak. This could change if the EU-3 could at least bluff the clerical regime into believing that they might consider draconian sanctions—but this seems very unlikely. The only real bright spot on the horizon is Grand Ayatollah [Ali] Sistani and the possibility of a Shiite-led democracy just across the border [in Iraq]. Ahmadinejad's election appears to have shaken Tehran's establishment. The new president, unlike the old, appears to be an unreconstructed socialist, who might actually make Iran's dirigiste [state-controlled] economy even worse. This is no mean achievement with oil prices sky-high—we should, of course, wish him well.

The only way Iran is going to get better is for it to get a lot worse—and Ahmadinejad may just possibly be the man to galvanize a broad-based opposition to the regime. Right now, he and Sistani are the only hopes we've got for convulsions and evolution inside Iran's clerical class. If the Bush administration were wise, it would start to speak about religious freedom in Iran and the ruling clergy's oppression of the more traditional clerics of the holy cities of Qom and Mashhad. If the Bush administration were serious, it would batter the CIA until it began the slow and difficult process of trying to make contact with the anti-Khamenei forces among Iran's mullahs. In all probability, irreversible evolution or regime crackup will be driven by clerical dissent, not by Iranian liberals, progressives, or others with whom counterrevolutionary American-Iranian expatriates are comfortable.

10

Military Force Is the Best Option for Dealing with Iran

Thomas Holsinger

Thomas Holsinger is an attorney in California.

The Iranian nuclear program is an extremely serious threat to the United States. A nuclear Iran would be able to support terrorists with impunity and might even give small nuclear weapons to those terrorist groups. Moreover, if Iran gets nuclear weapons, many other Middle Eastern countries will feel that they need nuclear weapons for their own security, increasing the chance that a terrorist group will get a nuclear bomb. The only way to protect the United States from the threat posed by the Iranian nuclear program is to invade the country and overthrow its government—soon, before it has functional nuclear weapons. The cost of an invasion may be high, but it would be more costly to cope with nuclear terrorism.

America has come to another turning point—whether our inaction will again engulf the world and us in a nightmare comparable to World War Two. This will entail loss of our freedom as the price of domestic security measures against terrorist weapons of mass destruction, though we might suffer nuclear attack before implementing those measures. The only

Thomas Holsinger, "The Case for Invading Iran," Windsofchange.net, January 19, 2006. Reproduced by permission.

effective alternative is American use of pre-emptive military force against an imminent threat—Iranian nuclear weapons, which requires that we invade Iran and overthrow its mullah regime as we did to Iraq's Baathist regime.

All the reasons for invading Iraq apply doubly to Iran, and with far greater urgency. Iran right now poses the imminent threat to America which Iraq did not in 2003. Iran may already have some nuclear weapons, purchased from North Korea or made with materials acquired from North Korea, which would increase its threat to us from imminent to direct and immediate.

The State of the Iranian Nuclear Program

Iran's mullahs are about to produce their first home-built nuclear weapons. . . . If we permit that, many other countries, some of whose governments are dangerously unstable, will build their own nuclear weapons to deter Iran and each other from nuclear attack as our inaction will have demonstrated our unwillingness to keep the peace. This rapid and widespread proliferation will inevitably lead to use of nuclear weapons in anger, both by terrorists and by fearful and unstable third world regimes, at which point the existing world order will break down and we will suffer every Hobbesian nightmare of nuclear proliferation.

Iran has dramatically shortened the time required to acquire the necessary weapons-grade fissionable materials by purchase abroad of pre-enriched, but not yet weapons-grade, fissionable materials (not just from North Korea). Iran's technicians already have the expertise to fabricate functional nuclear weapons. The latter opinion is held by, among others, Mohamed El Baradei, director-general of the United Nations' International Atomic Energy Agency, who said that Iran can produce nuclear weapons in a few months if it has the requisite weapons-grade fissionables: "And if they have the nuclear material and they have a parallel weaponization program along the way, they are really not very far—a few months—from a weapon."

It normally takes years to produce the highly purified fissionables required for nuclear weapons—that is the only obstacle after Pakistan let its nuclear weapons program director [A.Q. Khan] sell the knowledge of weapons fabrication to anyone with enough money. All estimates alleging that it will take Iran years to produce nuclear weapons assume that they will do so from scratch, but that is not the case. Iran purchased pre-enriched fissionables with the intent of "breaking out" in a short period to a fully stocked production "pipeline" of fissionables under enrichment at all stages of the process, from "yellowcake" at the low end to almost ready at the high end.

It is possible, and in my opinion has already happened, that Iran has purchased enough nuclear materials from North Korea to fabricate a few nuclear weapons and facilitate the following strategy. Iran could minimize the duration of a "window" of vulnerability to pre-emptive American or Israeli attack between their first nuclear tests (or announcement that they have nuclear weapons), and possession of enough nukes to deter attack, by postponing the announcement and/or first tests until they have a full-speed production line going— everything from enriching fissionables to weapons-grade and fabricating those into nuclear weapons, to stocks of finished nuclear weapons. At that point most or all of the latter will likely be of North Korean origin, but those will be quickly outnumbered by made-in-Iran ones under final assembly at the time of the announcement. I believe this is the plan Iran is following. . . .

The recent spike in world oil prices gave Iran's mullahs billions of dollars more in hard currency for use in acquiring material for their nuclear weapons program. The timing of their ongoing breakout to public nuclear weapons capability, and the public threats of Iran's president, indicate that some recent event has given them additional confidence here. I feel this was their purchase of enough nuclear weapons materials from North Korea to fabricate a few nuclear weapons. They might have bought fully operational North Korean nukes. Such North Korean complicity carries other implications.

Whatever the reason, Iran's mullahs no longer seem to feel a need to wait for final processing of fissionables, and fabrication of those into nuclear weapons, before their nuclear deterrent against the United States is ready. They act like they presently have that deterrent, and are proceeding to backfill their fissionable processing and weapons fabrication line before announcing that they have nuclear weapons. . . .

Iran's mullahs will use nuclear weapons as a shield against foreign attack while they more openly support terrorism elsewhere.

The Consequences of an Iranian Nuclear Deterrent

Those who have considered the consequences of Iran's open possession of nuclear weapons (as opposed to covert possession) have generally focused on its avowed threats against Israel and the United States. Those are certainly enough grounds for pre-emptive attack by both—Iran's mullah regime is the one government in the entire world whose possession of nuclear weapons would most pose a direct and immediate threat to America and Israel.

Iran's mullahs will use nuclear weapons as a shield against foreign attack while they more openly support terrorism elsewhere. American acquiescence in Iranian nuclear weapons will lose the war on terror by ceding terrorists a "privileged sanctuary" in Iran. We'll have let terrorists have in Iran what we invaded Iraq to stop. The invasion of Iraq will have been a complete waste of effort, and our dead in Iraq will have died in vain.

The chief threat of Iranian nukes, however, is what they will lead to elsewhere—something which will make all of the above trivial by comparison, something which will go on and on long after Iran's mullah regime is overthrown by the Iranian people.

If the United States does not forcibly prevent Iran from producing nuclear weapons, every country in the area will know to a moral certainty that they cannot rely on the United States for protection against Iranian nuclear attack, or Iranian nuclear blackmail in support of domestic opposition to the generally shaky regimes of the Middle East. American prestige and influence there will collapse. If we won't protect ourselves by pre-emption, we can't be relied on to protect anyone else.

So every country within reach of Iranian nuclear weapons will have enormous strategic pressure to develop their own nuclear weapons to deter Iranian nuclear threats. As a recent strategic survey noted, Syria has many times the per capita and absolute GDP [gross domestic product] of North Korea, and Egypt several times the per capita and absolute GDP of Pakistan. If North Korea and Pakistan can develop nuclear weapons, so can Syria and Egypt, and also Saudi Arabia, all three of whose regimes are shaky. And they won't be the only countries to develop nuclear weapons after Iran does—many more will join the nuclear "club" within a few years, some within months.

All of those countries having nuclear weapons will create a security nightmare—at some point terrorists will be able to buy or steal some (assuming that Iran doesn't first give a few to favored terrorist groups). It is likely that at least some will use their nuclear weapons on each other, or in a domestic coup or factional fight. The latter might first happen in Iran.

The Consequences of Nuclear Terrorism

Few have any idea of the degree to which international trade and prosperity relies on free movement of goods between countries. Container cargo is an ideal means of covertly transporting terrorist nuclear weapons. Once the first terrorist nuke is used, international trade will be enormously curtailed for at least several months for security reasons, and the entire world will suffer a simultaneous recession.

It won't stop there, though. These same security precautions, once implemented, will significantly impede future economic growth—a ballpark estimate of reducing worldwide growth by 20–30% is reasonable. Consider the worldwide and domestic effects over a twenty-year period of a one-quarter across the board reduction in economic growth.

This will be just from security precautions against terrorist nukes—not physical destruction from such use nor, more importantly, the consequences of nuclear wars between or within third world states. Physical destruction from these will be bad enough, but that pales compared with the social and consequent economic effects—enormous tides of refugees, economic collapse and outright anarchy over wide areas.

We cannot avoid that washing over us from abroad even if we manage to avoid terrorist nuclear attack at home, and we are unlikely to be so lucky. Scores if not hundreds of thousands of Americans will likely be killed, and many more injured, from terrorist nuclear devices used in America when so many politically unstable countries possess hundreds of the things.

We better than most can economically afford the thoroughly intrusive security measures required to protect against terrorist nukes when the threat can come from anywhere, as opposed to Islamic extremists alone.

But the price of domestic security, when foreign security fails due to a failure of leadership and will by President Bush, will be something much more precious—our freedom.

Freedom everywhere will suffer due to those same security precautions. The greatest loss of freedom will come in those countries which are freest, i.e., especially America. Especially us.

THIS is what is really at stake—the freedom which makes us Americans.

The Use of Force Is Necessary

It is obvious that Iran's leaders cannot be deterred from developing nuclear weapons. The U.N. won't stop them. Diplomatic solutions won't—the mullahs' bad faith is obvious. Their diplomacy serves the same purpose as Japan's with us in late 1941 after their carrier attack fleet had sailed for Pearl Harbor—to distract us from the coming attack. We are at that same point now, only we know the Kido Butai [Japanese strike force] is coming and have no excuse for surprise. Iran's President has openly stated their real intentions. Iranian diplomacy merely lets the willing deceive themselves.

There isn't time to overthrow Iran's mullah regime through subversion . . ., and President Bush's toleration of factional disputes in our national security apparatus means that we lack the capability to do so, period.

Iran seems to be in a pre-revolutionary state such that its mullah regime will collapse from purely domestic reasons within a few years even if we do nothing, but by then it will have openly had nuclear weapons for several years, possibly used them against Israel and/or been pre-emptively nuked by Israel, and widespread nuclear proliferation will have started with all the horrors that will bring.

Only military force [now] can prevent this nightmare. Bombing alone won't do it—it will only postpone things, and Iran's mullahs won't just sit there while we're bombing them. War is a two-way street. They have spent years preparing for this conflict, and will try to stop Persian Gulf oil exports. There will also be an instant massive uprising by Iranian-led Shiite militias in southern Iraq.

Half-measures in war only make things worse. If we really want to find out how much Iran's mullah regime can hurt us, and relearn the lessons of Vietnam, we need only bomb without invading. That will maximize our losses. Those who advocate mere bombing have not considered that Iran might already have some nuclear weapons.

The only effective way to stop the mullahs from building nukes, while minimizing our losses from their counter-attacks, is to overthrow their regime by invasion and conquest.

Israel does not have the military capability we do. Israeli air attack against Iran's dispersed and hardened nuclear facilities will at most postpone Iranian production by a few months. The United States Air Force can postpone it for as long as we keep up the attacks, but the mullahs will counterattack such that we'll be at war whether we want to be or not, only with no chance of victory while we're afraid to win.

The only effective way to stop the mullahs from building nukes, while minimizing our losses from their counter-attacks, is to overthrow their regime by invasion and conquest as we did against Saddam Hussein's regime in Iraq.

A War Against Iran Is Winnable

Democratic military experts agreed in a recent *Atlantic Monthly* article that eliminating Iran's mullah regime with a ground invasion is feasible—they were more optimistic about it than I am (my emphasis):

> In all their variety, these and other regime-change plans he described had two factors in common. One is that they minimized "stability" efforts—everything that would happen after the capital fell. "We want to take out of this operation what has caused us problems in Iraq," Gardiner of CentCom said, referring to the postwar morass. "The idea is to give the President an option that he can execute that will *involve about twenty days of buildup that will probably not be seen by the world. Thirty days of operation to regime change*

and taking down the nuclear system, and little or no stability operations. Our objective is to be on the outskirts of Tehran in about two weeks. The notion is we will not have a Battle of Tehran; we don't want to do that. We want to have a battle around the city. We want to bring our combat power to the vicinity of Tehran and use Special Operations to take the targets inside the capital. We have no intention of getting bogged down in stability options in Iran afterwards. Go in quickly, change the regime, find a replacement, and get out quickly after having destroyed—rendered inoperative—the nuclear facilities."

I believe the durations mentioned in the *Atlantic* article should be at least doubled—it won't take us only 7–10 more days to overthrow Iran's regime than it did Iraq's, not to mention locating and destroying the known and secret nuclear facilities scattered over a wide area. I feel the *Atlantic* panel significantly underestimated logistic problems. Our forces must pass through mountains to get to Iran's capital of Tehran, while getting to Baghdad required passage only through deserts and broad river valleys. Iran is much bigger than Iraq, so our ground forces will have a greater distance to travel, while even minor resistance in mountain passes will cause significant delays.

The *Atlantic* article concluded that eliminating the mullah regime was feasible—we agree that Iranian ground resistance will be minor, especially compared to our forces' extreme effectiveness—but the *Atlantic* panelists felt that the consequences had too high a price. I agree that the occupation campaign afterwards will be much worse for us, in terms of intensity and required manpower, than the occupation campaign in Iraq—they felt the necessary manpower required for several years' occupation duty would be prohibitive. They did not, however, even attempt to weigh that against the consequences of letting Iran have nuclear weapons, the effects of it already having some, and the probable duration of an occupation campaign. I do. The tradeoffs between the cost of an extended occupation in Iran, and its desirability, change dramatically if we must search for easily concealed, ready-to-use nuclear weapons, as opposed to merely destroying the physical ability to produce them.

I also feel the occupation campaign in Iran will take much less time than the one in Iraq for the following reasons:

1. Iran has a functioning civil society and democratic tradition while Iraq didn't. The mullahs veto candidates they don't like, more in the past few years than earlier, but the systems and mindset for a functioning democratic society are present.

2. We can use many of the Iranian army's junior officers, non-commissioned officers and enlisted personnel as a cadre for the new democratic regime's security forces. We couldn't do that with Iraq's army as the officers and non-coms were almost exclusively Sunni Arabs, a.k.a. Baathist regime loyalists, and the mostly Shiite conscripts had almost all gone home.

3. Iran has at least one order of magnitude, and probably several orders of magnitude, less loose explosives than were present in Iraq, for possible use in improvised explosive devices. The mullah regime die-hards will die much faster than the Baathist die-hards in Iraq, because the ones in Iran will be attacking our forces mostly with direct-fire weapons. That is suicidal against American forces.

4. Language and ethnicity differences mean that Al Qaeda's purely Sunni foreign terrorists won't be able to operate much in Iran. The latter operated only briefly in Shiite areas of Iraq—those that didn't leave quickly died horribly at Shiite hands. While there are a lot of Sunnis in Iran, few of those are Arabs—they're Kurds, Azeris, etc.

My rough estimate of American casualties in the conquest and occupation campaigns for Iran, assuming that the mullahs don't nuke us, or use chemical weapons, is that we'd take about 50% more casualties in the first 18–24 months in Iran than in three years in Iraq, mostly in the twelve month period after the initial conquest.

I agree with the *Atlantic* panelists that the conquest campaign in Iran would, in terms of casualties, cost little more than Iraq's—several hundred allied KIA [killed in action]. I just think it would take longer.

Everyone I know of with opinions on the subject agrees that the occupation campaign in Iran would be more intense than Iraq's, but Iraq's has seen only about 1700 KIA (or is it total fatalities including accidents?) during the 33 months of the occupation to date. That is about 50 fatalities per month for an average of about 120,000 troops (1 fatality per month per 2400 troops).

If Iran's occupation entails 200,000 men and is twice as intense as Iraq's in terms of casualties, we're looking at 1 fatality per 1200 men per month. 200k x 12 months = 2400k divided by 1200 = 2000 fatalities per year. This is certainly a lot compared to Iraq's occupation campaign, but it also indicates that American casualties in Iran will be acceptable by any reasonable standard.

In my opinion the occupation campaign in Iran will be awful only for the first year, and then conditions will improve much faster than in Iraq for reasons mentioned above in this post. My guesstimate at this point is about 3000 American fatalities over two years for both the conquest and occupation campaigns in Iran, though the first year would be ghastly.

That Iran may already have some nuclear weapons (in my opinion this is likely) complicates a prospective invasion. We'd had a plan for several years to destroy Iran's nuclear weapons capability (i.e., the launchers as well as the warheads)—it is called variously "Global Strike" and CONPLAN 8022. The United States Air Force [USAF] excels at blowing things up.

Consider also, that, if small numbers of Iranian nuclear weapons are enough of a threat to seriously menace an American invasion, they are enough of a threat to merit pre-emptive attack with American nuclear weapons. Get real—our nukes are bigger than theirs, and we have lots more than they do. And if Iranian nuclear weapons aren't enough of a threat to merit pre-emptive use of our own, they're not a reason to avoid invading. It is not likely, however, that the USAF will need nuclear weapons to keep the mullahs from getting any off.

Fear of possible Iranian nuclear weapons use against an American invasion is not a valid reason for doing nothing.

Did I mention the bribes? Now is the time for some breathtaking bribes—say a billion dollars per Iranian nuke delivered to us, which would be cheap given the alternative. Once we demonstrate the will to invade and eliminate the mullah regime, such bribes would be more effective than most think. Psychological warfare was wildly successful in the invasion of Iraq.

Fear of possible Iranian nuclear weapons use against an American invasion is not a valid reason for doing nothing. A thousand more American civilians have been killed by enemy action at home in this war than American servicemen killed at home and abroad. Not invading Iran will increase this disparity by several orders of magnitude. We have armed forces to protect our civilians from the enemy, not vice versa—soldiers die so civilians don't. We will invade Iran to protect the American people from nuclear attack. That is worth the risk posed by Iranian nuclear weapons to American soldiers, and the burden of deploying 200,000 troops there for several years. Our reserves knew when they enlisted that they'd be called up for the duration of a major war. Invasion of Iran to protect

America from nuclear attack, and preserve our freedom, counts as a major war.

This would, however, make absolute hash of the Bush administration's quite fictitious future budget estimates, which are the reason why it refused to significantly expand our ground forces after 9/11 though such was obviously necessary. Those phony budget estimates are arguably the biggest obstacle to our invasion of Iran [any time soon]. Iran's mullahs might even have counted on this in timing their breakout to public nuclear weapons possession.

11

Covert Action Could Be Used to Deal with the Iranian Nuclear Threat

Terrence Henry

Terrence Henry is a journalist with the Atlantic Monthly.

A campaign of covert action, carried out by Western intelligence services, may be one way to end the nuclear threat from Iran. Such a campaign could include intercepting shipments of critical nuclear equipment before they reach Iran, sabotaging machinery destined for Iran's nuclear facilities, or assassinating Iranian nuclear scientists. Similar covert campaigns have been successfully used to slow down a country's nuclear program before, and enough sabotage-caused setbacks could even convince Iran to abandon the program altogether.

In the debate over how to respond to Iran's pursuit of nuclear weapons, much attention has been paid to the "Osirak option"—a reference to Israel's successful 1981 air strike on Iraq's Osirak reactor, which was then on the verge of producing plutonium for a nuclear weapon. Considerably less has been said about the seemingly star-crossed history of the reactor, and those involved with it, in the years before the bombing.

Terrence Henry, "The Covert Option: Can Sabotage and Assassination Stop Iran from Going Nuclear?" *Atlantic Monthly*, vol. 296, December 2005, p. 54. Reproduced by permission of the author.

The Osirak Covert Action Campaign

Iraq bought the cores for the Osirak reactor from France. Originally they were to be shipped to Iraq in April of 1979, but shortly before their departure an explosion ripped through the warehouse that held them. An organization calling itself the French Ecological Group, which had never been heard of before (and hasn't been heard from since), claimed responsibility. Shipment was delayed for six months while the cores were repaired.

When diplomatic efforts have begun to fail but an overt military strike is not yet politically or operationally feasible, covert action becomes attractive.

The next year Yahya al-Meshad, an important scientist in Iraq's nuclear program, arrived in France to test fuel for the reactor. The morning he was to return home a maid entered his Paris hotel room and found that he had been stabbed and bludgeoned to death. (The only person known to have seen the scientist the previous night, a prostitute who called herself Marie Express, was killed a few weeks later in a hit-and-run accident. The culprit was never found.) Soon afterward workers at firms supplying parts for the reactor began to receive threatening letters from a mysterious group called the Committee to Safeguard the Islamic Revolution. Bombs went off at the offices of one of the firms, in Italy, and at the home of the company's director-general. Over the next several months two more Iraqi nuclear scientists died in separate poisoning incidents. It is of course unlikely that these events were coincidental; most experts today believe that Mossad—Israel's secret service—was behind each of them, though it has never claimed responsibility.

It wouldn't be the first time Israel turned to sabotage or assassination to deter another country from obtaining nuclear weapons or the missiles to deliver them, and if the current standoff with Iran persists, it may not be the last. When diplomatic efforts have begun to fail but an overt military strike is not yet politically or operationally feasible, covert action becomes attractive. Israel and perhaps the United States are likely to pursue it against the Iranian nuclear program over the next few years if current attempts to negotiate a solution with Iran fall apart.

Methods of Sabotage

How might such a campaign play out? Iran's nuclear program relies on foreign companies for many crucial parts, as Iraq's did. A natural first target for disruption would be supply lines for these parts. Indeed, Jon Wolfsthal, a fellow at the Center for Strategic and International Studies, says that shipments of materials related to nuclear-weapons development have probably already "found their way to the bottom of the ocean." "Fires break out on board," Wolfsthal says. "Ships sink. If the U.S. or Israel came across intelligence that a ship registered in Singapore was going to deliver vacuum pumps [required for uranium enrichment] to a company in Dubai, those intelligence services would see to it that the boat didn't reach its destination." Supplies can also be rigged to damage the machinery in which they are installed, in transit or beforehand. Or working parts can be bugged to provide intelligence on where and how they are being used.

Even if Iran succeeds in acquiring all the supplies it needs (and it may be nearing that point), its nuclear program will remain vulnerable to sabotage. Producing fissile uranium is difficult and time-consuming, and the machinery required to do it is extremely sensitive. One step in the process is conversion, in which the uranium is blended with other chemicals and turned into a gas. In Iran this is reportedly taking place almost exclusively at the large Isfahan facility outside Tehran—a prime target for covert action. Theoretically, disabling the plant would not require especially clever tactics.

(Summoning the political will and operational capacity for such action is another matter.) According to Reuel Marc Gerecht, a former CIA [Central Intelligence Agency] officer who worked on Iran, a heavy backpack filled with plastic explosives would be enough to severely damage or destroy it.

If the process of turning uranium into a gas were not disrupted, the uranium would still need to be enriched. Iran's enrichment facilities most likely use old technology (provided by Pakistan) that is notoriously temperamental. "In our industry," Wolfsthal says, "we call these 'self-disassembling' machines." Enrichment takes place in long cascades of centrifuges; powerful magnets hold each centrifuge in place while it spins at high speeds to separate the fissile uranium. The magnets are prone to mishap. "If the [electrical] current powering the magnets fluctuates," Wolfsthal points out, "you can send the centrifuge flying out of its case, careening across the room like a bowling pin, and knocking out the rest of the centrifuge cascades." Such a fluctuation could be set off in the part of the power grid supplying the plant. (Like many other countries, Iran has a grid known to be unreliable at times and vulnerable to attack.) Similarly, letting a small amount of air into the vacuum-sealed centrifuges could destroy many of them and set the enrichment program back years.

Intimidation or Assassination

Building and operating Iran's nuclear program also requires the expertise of scientists and technicians. Intimidating or assassinating key scientists has forestalled weapons development in other countries. In the late 1950s Egypt launched a ballistic-missile program with the help of German scientists, many of whom were former Nazis. In July of 1962 [Egyptian] President Gamal Abdel Nasser unveiled two new test missiles at a military parade, bragging that they could hit targets "south of Beirut." Mossad quickly responded with Operation Damocles, an intimidation campaign targeting the

German scientists. One scientist was killed in September, two months after the parade, and in the following months the scientists' families were threatened directly. In November several letter bombs addressed to the scientists were sent to the rocket facilities in Egypt; one of them killed five Egyptians. (This part of the campaign was rumored to have been called "post-mortem.") Soon all the German scientists had left Egypt—and its missile program—behind. Without them the program withered.

Iran's indigenous scientific capabilities today are much greater than Egypt's were in the 1960s, so presumably it would be much harder to eliminate them—but perhaps not impossible. A recent report written by several former senior Israeli military and intelligence officials under the leadership of Dr. Louis Beres, an American professor of international relations and international law at Purdue, advises [Israel] to adopt a "doctrine of pre-emption" against Iran's nuclear program, and provides a menu of covert and overt options for crippling it. Prominent among them is "decapitation"—a swift covert strike against either the "enemy leadership elites" or the program's scientists and engineers. Several experts are skeptical that such a plan could succeed. But Beres believes that the logistical hurdles are surmountable. "The question," he says, "is to what extent this would be regarded as barbarous, uncivilized, and destabilizing by the international community."

Potential Outcomes

Covert action alone is unlikely to solve the problem of Iranian nuclear ambitions. After all, the cloak-and-dagger efforts to sabotage the Osirak reactor bought only a couple of years' delay before Israel launched a military strike. But some of Iran's nuclear facilities (like Natanz) are not as close to being fully operational as Osirak was in 1981, and in some ways its program is more vulnerable. And permanent solutions look hard to come by today.

Meanwhile, both the United States and Israel are deeply concerned that Iran, with a nuclear shield to defend it, might seek to expand its influence as it did in the years immediately following the Islamic revolution, when it used [extremist] groups like Hizbollah and Palestinian Islamic Jihad to carry out large-scale terrorist attacks in the region. The Israelis worry that Iran would resume attacks against their country through these terrorist groups after a ten-year period of relative quiet.

By reducing the Iranians' confidence in their ability to produce nuclear weapons, [a covert action campaign] might even prompt Iran to consider abandoning its nuclear program.

Ashton Carter, a former assistant secretary of defense, says that he would be "surprised and disappointed" if a covert campaign wasn't already under way. Conducted skillfully, Carter argues, such a campaign might not merely forestall Iranian progress toward a bomb; it might also sow doubt, causing Iranian officials to question whether their equipment actually worked and whether the people involved in the program could be trusted. By reducing the Iranians' confidence in their ability to produce nuclear weapons, it might even prompt Iran to consider abandoning its nuclear program, in return for the carrots it has so far spurned at the negotiating table.

12

Encouraging an Internal Revolution Is a Viable Option for Dealing with Iran

Ilan Berman

Ilan Berman is the vice president for policy of the American Foreign Policy Council, a think tank based in Washington, D.C. He is also an adjunct faculty member in international relations at the National Defense University and American University.

The United States should put more money and effort into reaching out to the people of Iran through public diplomacy, such as radio and television broadcasts and academic and cultural exchange programs. These sorts of programs were instrumental in bringing about the fall of communism in Russia and Eastern Europe. The size and funding of such programs, however, have been cut sharply since the Cold War, despite the fact that such a public diplomacy program is clearly needed to improve America's image in the Muslim world. Many young Iranians do not support their current government, and the Iranian people are the most pro-American in the Middle East. Therefore such efforts have a high chance of encouraging the Iranian people to demand democracy in their country.

During the fall of 2002, a remarkable event took place in Iran. The country's parliament, or *majles*, in an effort to capitalize on the wave of anti-Americanism sweeping the region, and as a way of shoring up its own anti-Western policies, commissioned an official poll to survey national attitudes toward the United States. The outcome was supposed to be predetermined—a resounding vote in favor of Tehran's continued antagonism toward Washington, and a renewed mandate for the Islamic Revolution at home and abroad.

But Iran's leaders found out that they should be careful what they wish for. Fully 74 percent of the approximately 1,500 Iranians surveyed by three different polling institutes, including Iran's quasi-official National Institute for Research Studies and Opinion Polls, supported the idea of dialogue with the United States. And less than eight months after President [George W.] Bush had labeled their country part of an "Axis of Evil," nearly half of those polled affirmed that Washington's policy toward Iran was "to some extent correct." All in all, it was a resounding defeat for Iran's ruling theocracy.

The results of the September 2002 survey provide a telling glimpse into the sorry state of affairs within Iran. Just over two and a half decades after the Islamic Revolution, the country is nothing short of a failed state. Half of its sixty-nine million population lives below the poverty line. A fifth is unemployed, and 1.4 million youths join its ranks every year. Inflation stands at around 25 percent, while per capita income is at pre-Revolutionary levels (some $1,800 per year). Corruption has decayed virtually every sector of the government and the economy. Prostitution and drug abuse are rampant, with teenage addiction rates five times higher than those of the United States.

Moreover, conditions worsened under the rule of Mohammed Khatami. Despite his public calls for domestic reforms and a "dialogue of civilizations" with the West, Iran's "reformist" president presided over a full-bore assault on freedom of expression and political dissent. Since 2001, the Iranian regime has shut down more than one hundred newspapers and imprisoned dozens of opposition journalists. This led the international media watchdog Reporters Without Borders, in its 2004 annual report, to dub Iran "the biggest prison for journalists in the Middle East." At the same time, numerous pieces of legislation passed by the *majles*—on such topics as judicial freedoms, police procedures, and international humanitarian standards—remain unratified. These conditions led the UN General Assembly to formally express "serious concern" about the "continuing violations of human rights" in Iran in December 2004.

Between March 2002 and March 2003, more than a thousand anti-regime protests are estimated to have taken place throughout Iran.

It is perhaps not surprising, therefore, that the country's political consensus has begun to crumble. In July 2002, the Ayatollah Jalaleddin Taheri, a stalwart of the old regime, unexpectedly resigned from his post as the Imam of Isfahan. Taheri's letter of resignation, circulated widely in the Iranian press, blasted the "failed" policies of the current regime for the country's "unemployment, inflation and high prices, the hellish gap between poverty and wealth, the deep and daily-growing distance between the classes, the stagnation and decline of national revenue, a sick economy, bureaucratic corruption, desperately weak administrators, the growing flaws in the country's political structure, embezzlement, bribery and addiction." Taheri is not alone; other Iranian clerics and intellectuals have since followed suit, publicly breaking with the policies of the regime in Tehran to call for a new national political balance.

Even the regime's enforcers no longer seem to be immune from doubts. In February 2003, the London-based *Al Sharq al-Awsat* disclosed that three top Iranian security officials had recently defected from the Islamic Republic, taking with them a trove of documents, video recordings, and personnel files. Those who have stayed, meanwhile, appear increasingly disaffected. During the student protests that shook Iran in the summer of 2003, the regime was forced to recruit hundreds of Arab mercenaries for their clampdown on dissent. Apparently, Tehran's mullahs can no longer even trust the loyalty of their own enforcers.

Just as significantly, Iran is in the throes of a demographic and ideological upheaval. Fully two-thirds of the Iranian population is under the age of thirty, and half is under age twenty. Most Iranians, therefore, have lived nearly all of their lives under the Islamic Revolution, and are painfully aware of its shortcomings. Not coincidentally, they are among the only truly pro-American populations in the region. In the days after 9/11, as throngs celebrated in other parts of the Muslim world, hundreds of Iranians took to the streets to express their solidarity with the United States. They did so again in November 2002, in a nationwide series of student protests with many manifestations but one unifying theme: "Death to the Taliban, in Kabul and in Tehran." The scope of this opposition is breathtaking. Between March 2002 and March 2003, more than a thousand anti-regime protests are estimated to have taken place throughout Iran.

Communication Breakdown

For the United States, Iran's youthful, pro-Western population represents an indispensable constituency. After all, one of the Bush administration's most enduring challenges in the War on Terror has been effectively communicating its goals and objectives to a skeptical Muslim world. Since 9/11, this imperative has spawned a frenetic American public diplomacy effort—including media outreach by top administration officials—aimed at winning hearts and minds in the Middle East.

Yet Iran has figured only belatedly in these plans. More than nine months after September 11th, [2001,] and with American officials appearing repeatedly on Arabic networks like *al-Jazeera*, not one high-ranking U.S. official had yet attempted to make the case for the "Bush Doctrine" on Iranian radio or television, despite the availability of numerous foreign broadcasting outlets capable of effectively carrying their message.

Even when the U.S. government did finally attempt to correct this omission, the results fell far short of adequate. In December 2002, with much fanfare, the U.S. Broadcasting Board of Governors launched its new 24-hour-a-day Farsi-language broadcasting vehicle, *Radio Farda*. Quickly, however, the station's entertainment-driven format unleashed a barrage of criticism. The United States, observers in both the Congress and the media said, had diluted its democratic message. Since then, broadcasting to Iran has languished, despite Congressional attempts to expand outreach.

The lackluster nature of this effort is symptomatic of a larger malaise within the U.S. government—confusion about exactly whom within the Iranian regime to engage. Ever since Khatami's May 1997 election, hopes for contact with more moderate elements of Tehran's clerical establishment have persisted in official Washington. These yearnings have squelched any real progress in the quest for alternatives to the current regime in Tehran. Iran's ayatollahs, for their part, have nurtured this inertia, permitting the veneer of pluralism (but no real progress) in Iran's domestic political debate. The result? No American strategy, and a policy vulnerable to Tehran's manipulation.

Such disarray can have devastating consequences. This became clear in the summer of 2003, when a renewed resurgence of anti-regime protests rocked the Islamic Republic. Over the course of several weeks, thousands of protesters took to the streets of Tehran and other Iranian cities, rallied by foreign broadcasting outlets like the Los Angeles-based National Iranian Television (NITV). Unable to curtail such foreign broadcasting itself, Iran turned to Fidel Castro's Cuba. Within days, Havana began using a Russian-built electronic warfare facility to jam both U.S. government and private broadcasts into the Islamic Republic. The interference eliminated a crucial outlet for political information and organization for Iranian protesters, effectively neutralizing the nascent democratic protests at a critical time, when they had begun spreading across the country. A stunned American official likened the jamming to an "act of war."

Yet a robust American response failed to materialize. The administration brushed aside the significance of the satellite jamming, and did nothing to demonstrate to Iran's ayatollahs—and to their comrades-in-arms abroad—that such interference carries serious consequences. In the process, Washington telegraphed a distinct message: there are limits to America's support of the Iranian people's urge for democracy.

The Reagan Doctrine Revisited

Reversing this trend requires the United States to utilize public diplomacy as part of a larger political warfare strategy—one designed to engage and empower the Iranian population vis-à-vis the clerical regime.

Such an idea is not new. During the Cold War, the United States relied heavily on public diplomacy, via organs like the Voice of America, the United States Information Agency (USIA), and Radio Free Europe, to pierce the Iron Curtain and export American ideals to the Soviet Bloc. Perhaps the most ardent proponent of this war of ideas against the U.S.S.R. was President Ronald Reagan. On his watch, efforts to spread American values abroad were strengthened significantly through the creation of new institutions like the National Endowment for Democracy and new broadcasting outlets such as Radio Marti [targeting Cuba], as well as through major infusions of funding.

Close to a year and a half after September 11, the United States was still spending . . . about one-third less on public diplomacy than it did during the Cold War.

The results were dramatic. At the height of their Cold War popularity, America's premier public diplomacy vehicles—the Voice of America, Radio Free Europe, and Radio Liberty—reached up to 80 percent of the population of Eastern Europe, and half of the citizens of the Soviet Union, every week. And the message they carried empowered, inspired, and motivated a generation of leaders in the Soviet Bloc, ranging from Czechoslovakia's future president, Vaclav Havel, to the U.S.S.R.'s most prominent dissident and Nobel Laureate, Andrei Sakharov. The direct impact of American public diplomacy was visible in such places as Poland, where U.S. support spurred the emergence of Lech Walesa's *Solidarnosc* (Solidarity) movement in the early 1980s.

Since the end of the Cold War, however, the United States has all but abdicated public diplomacy as a vehicle by which to engage the outside world. Through a series of steps during the 1990s—from steep cuts for broadcast staffing funds to the reduction of cultural exchange programs—America's tools of outreach were systematically eviscerated and politicized. The culmination came in October 1999, with the formal elimination of the USIA as a freestanding governmental agency as part of new legislation aimed at restructuring and streamlining the nation's public diplomacy effort.

More than half a decade later, this trend has not been reversed. When surveyed close to a year and a half after September 11th, the United States was still spending, in real terms, about one-third less on public diplomacy than it did during the Cold War—notwithstanding an acute need to inform a massive base of "undecided" citizens in the Arab and Muslim world about American objectives and values. Just as significantly, the message of American public diplomacy has effectively been neutered through programmatic changes that have placed a premium on popular music (and a smattering of news reporting) at the expense of hard-hitting democracy coverage designed to empower and educate listeners the world over. These sad facts led President Bush's blue-ribbon panel on public diplomacy, chaired by former U.S. Ambassador to Syria Edward Djerejian, to charge in its October 2003 report that

> a process of unilateral disarmament in the weapons of advocacy over the last decade has contributed to widespread hostility toward Americans and left us vulnerable to lethal threats to our interests and our safety. In this time of peril, public diplomacy is absurdly and dangerously underfunded.

As this and numerous other studies on U.S. public diplomacy concluded since September 11th have made clear, American efforts need a renewed strategic direction, additional resources and, most of all, a serious commitment to winning the battle of ideas in the larger War on Terror. And there is no better place to start than Iran, a country in the midst of massive demographic and ideological change. With the proper political will, the United States has the ability to quickly generate a robust, effective public diplomacy effort aimed at empowering Iran's young, Western-looking population.

Practical Steps

In practical terms, doing so requires:

Expanding and optimizing existing outreach. In 2004, broadcasting to Iran accounted for about 2.5 percent of the entire $577 million budget of the U.S. Broadcasting Board of Governors (BBG), and just over 1 percent of the combined $1.17 billion public diplomacy budget of the State Department and the BBG. Put another way, the United States spends under twenty-two cents *per Iranian per year* on outreach to the Islamic Republic—less than one-third of what the U.S. was spending per capita on broadcasting into the Soviet Bloc two decades ago.

These meager resources fail to properly appreciate Iran's geopolitical importance, and the fact that broadcasting into the Islamic Republic requires an entirely new language set and different regional/cultural expertise than analogous efforts directed toward the Arab countries of the region. Both facts dictate that the United States should match its political interest in Iranian democracy with the financial investment necessary to make its outreach as effective as possible.

A reconfiguration of programming is also in order. Hard-hitting political analysis and coverage of current events currently account for one-quarter or less of the regular programming on America's premier public diplomacy outlet to the Islamic Republic, *Radio Farda*. The rest is taken up by lengthy broadcasts of popular music. Such a schedule is surely designed to appeal to Iran's young, Western-oriented population—an audience base that now numbers close to fifty million. Yet it would be a safe bet to say that a good portion of these young Iranians, struggling to define themselves under the corrupt, dictatorial rule of the regime in Tehran, want to hear about freedoms and personal liberties at least as much as they yearn for the latest *Top 40* offerings. The United States should make it a priority to allow them to do so.

Financing external broadcasting sources. In its quest to win Iranian hearts and minds, the United States has a powerful ally on its side: the Iranian expatriate community. The Persian diaspora in the United States now stands at over two million, making it the largest such Iranian community in the world. Over time, this vibrant, politically active segment of the U.S. population has charted substantial public diplomacy gains of its own in Iran via outlets like NITV and KRSI "Radio Sedaye Iran," located in Beverly Hills.

So far, the U.S. government has done little to shore up these independent voices. In fact, when efforts to do so have emerged—notably, in the form of legislation like the 2003 "Iran Democracy Act" proposed by Senator Sam Brownback (R-KS)—they have fallen victim to legislative infighting and conflicting political agendas. These failures constitute a critical oversight, since the broadcasting efforts of Iranian expatriate elements have proven to be more effective than anything the United States has brought to bear on the public diplomacy front vis-à-vis Iran (in part by virtue of their known and beloved newscasters, actors, and entertainers, who are household names in Iran, and are certainly viewed by Iranians as more politically independent than employees of the U.S. government). This is a lapse the administration should rectify in short order.

Funding complementary public diplomacy and political warfare mechanisms. If the high-profile organs of American public diplomacy like Voice of America and Radio Free Europe have declined in stature and reach since the end of the Cold War, subsidiary initiatives have fared even worse. Between 1991 and 2001, the number of academic and cultural exchanges between the United States and foreign nations was slashed by nearly 40 percent (from 45,000 to 29,000 annually) and the profile of American information centers abroad was scaled down dramatically. All this has taken its toll, leaving the United States unable to effectively counteract the negative media image of America that now permeates Arabic broadcasting (like the Doha-based *Al-Jazeera* and Hezbollah's dedicated *Al-Manar* television station) at the grassroots level. And the likelihood of a repeat performance of the Cold War successes of such programs—which exposed leaders like [former Egyptian president] Anwar Sadat and [former German chancellor] Helmut Kohl to the American message early in their political careers, and helped to instill in them an understanding of U.S. values—has been substantially reduced.

The resuscitation of such initiatives toward Iran is especially vital, given the age of the Iranian population and their increasingly evident discontent with the current clerical regime. Exposure to the American message, and to their counterparts in the United States, via cultural outreach and delegation visits could help further loosen the ideological bonds between the Iranian people and Iran's ayatollahs.

A concerted American public diplomacy campaign will . . . serve as a catalyst for change among the Islamic Republic's increasingly restive population.

In order to increase its effectiveness, direct public broadcasting should also be buttressed by practical measures aimed at engaging the Islamic Republic's nascent democratic opposition. These steps—from the dissemination of pro-American literature and audio recordings to the provision of resources for hard-hitting opposition research and reporting on the human rights abuses of the current regime—would allow the United States to communicate more effectively with opponents of Tehran's bankrupt clerical rule, give those same elements greater international voice, and help them to network among themselves at home and abroad.

Deterring foreign interference. As its summer 2003 collaboration with Cuba eloquently demonstrated, Iran today is aided by a number of international partners who have a stake in preserving the current regime's hold on power. To these nations, Washington must demonstrate, both in word and in deed, that meddling with American public diplomacy toward the Islamic Republic will not be tolerated, and will prompt serious political and economic consequences. Only by deterring outside interference with its public diplomacy (via diplomatic, political, and economic measures, including biting sanctions if necessary) can the United States hope to empower sustainable, long-term resistance to the regime in Tehran.

There is sound basis to expect success. After all, Iran is not North Korea, a "hermit kingdom" with few tangible and durable links to the outside world. On the whole, Iranians are well educated, politically sophisticated, and socially informed. A concerted American public diplomacy campaign will provide a much-needed sign that the United States is committed to democracy in Iran, and serve as a catalyst for change among the Islamic Republic's increasingly restive population. . . .

Clear, unequivocal support of Iran's opposition forces in their resistance to the current regime . . . could decisively tip the scales in favor of democracy in the Islamic Republic.

A Vision of Victory

Ever since its publication in September 2002, the Bush administration's National Security Strategy has generated an extraordinary amount of controversy. Critics of White House policy from across the political spectrum have attacked the soundness of the document's strategic centerpiece, the doctrine of preemption, and raised questions about its first practical application, the war in Iraq. Yet it is in another arena entirely—that of democracy promotion—that the "Bush doctrine" could have its most far-reaching successes. "The United States," the National Security Strategy proudly proclaims, "must defend liberty and justice because these principles are right and true for all people everywhere. No nation owns these aspirations, and no nation is exempt from them."

America must stand firmly for the nonnegotiable demands of human dignity: the rule of law; limits on the absolute power of the state; free speech; freedom of worship; equal justice; respect for women; religious and ethnic tolerance; and respect for private property. . . . Embodying lessons from our past and using the opportunity we have today, the national security strategy of the United States must start from these core beliefs and look outward for possibilities to expand liberty.

Nowhere is such an approach more desperately needed, or more attainable, than in Iran. For the Islamic Republic today resembles nothing quite so much as the Soviet Union in the final, dismal days of the Cold War. Clear unequivocal support of Iran's opposition forces in their resistance to the current regime—and the provision of the needed political backing and economic resources to empower their struggle—could decisively tip the scales in favor of democracy in the Islamic Republic.

The stakes are enormous. Not only would a change of the Iranian system constitute the greatest victory yet in the U.S.-led War on Terror, it would also dovetail with the aspirations of the vast majority of Iranians. In the words of one astute observer of Iranian politics, "[t]he geopolitical interests of the United States coincide with the interests of the majority of Iranians: a fundamental change in the nature of the regime in Tehran. The overthrow of the Islamic Republic of Iran is good for America and good for the Iranian people."

Such a convergence should be a tantalizing possibility for an administration that, in its formative strategy document, has proclaimed its commitment to promoting "a balance of power that favors freedom."

Organizations to Contact

American Enterprise Institute for Public Policy Research (AEI)
1150 Seventeenth St. NW, Washington, DC   20036
(202) 862-5800 • fax: (202) 862-7177
Web site: www.aei.org

AEI is a conservative think tank that studies both foreign and domestic policy. It maintains an extensive archive of short publications relating to international affairs and defense issues on its Web site. AEI's print publications include the bimonthly magazine *American Enterprise* and numerous books, including *Eternal Iran: Continuity and Chaos* by Michael Rubin and Patrick Clawson.

American Iranian Council (AIC)
20 Nassau St., Suite 111, Princeton, NJ   08542
(609) 252-9099 • fax: (609) 525-9698
e-mail: aic@american-iranian.org
Web site: www.american-iranian.org

AIC is a nonpartisan organization that seeks to improve U.S.-Iran relations by encouraging dialogue and constructive engagement between the countries and by educating Americans about Iran. AIC also advocates for democratic reform and respect for human rights in Iran. Its publications include the journal *AIC Insight* and the electronic newsletter *AIC Update*, both of which are archived on the council's Web site.

Brookings Institution
1775 Massachusetts Ave. NW, Washington, DC   20036-2188
(202) 797-6000 • fax: (202) 797-6004
e-mail: brookinfo@brookings.edu
Web site: www.brookings.edu

Founded in 1927, the institution is a liberal research and education organization that publishes material on economics, government, and foreign policy. It strives to serve as a bridge between scholarship and public policy, bringing new knowledge to the attention of decision makers and providing scholars with insight into public policy issues. Its many publications include the quarterly *Brookings Review* and the Policy Briefs series of papers.

Carnegie Endowment for International Peace

1779 Massachusetts Ave. NW, Washington, DC 20036
(202) 483-7600 • fax: (202) 483-1840
e-mail: info@ceip.org
Web site: www.ceip.org

The Carnegie Endowment for International Peace was founded in 1910 in order to bring about an end to international warfare. The endowment has continued to conduct research on international affairs and U.S. foreign policy with the aim of finding cooperative solutions to international problems. Its publications include numerous policy briefs on foreign affairs, available for free on its Web site, and the quarterly journal *Foreign Policy*.

Center for Nonproliferation Studies

Monterey Institute for International Studies, Monterey, CA 93940
(831) 647-4154 • fax: (831) 238-9604
Web site: http://cns.miis.edu

The center researches all aspects of nonproliferation and works to combat the spread of weapons of mass destruction. The center produces research databases and makes papers and other materials dealing with the Iranian nuclear program available online. Its main publication is the *Nonproliferation Review*, which is published three times per year.

Center for Strategic & International Studies (CSIS)

1800 K St. NW, Washington, DC 20006
(202) 887-0200 • fax: (202) 775-3199
Web site: www.csis.org

The center is a bipartisan think tank that conducts research into U.S. defense and security policies, global challenges, and the political and economic transformations of foreign countries. Its International Security Program has been active in trying to develop a cooperative diplomatic effort to prevent Iran from getting nuclear weapons. CSIS's publications include numerous reports and white papers.

Council on Foreign Relations
58 E. Sixty-eighth St., New York, NY   10021
(212) 434-9400 • fax: (212) 986-2984
Web site: www.cfr.org

The council is a nonpartisan resource for information on and analysis of international issues. It specializes in foreign affairs, studying the international aspects of American political and economic policies and problems. Articles and op-ed pieces by council members are available on its Web site, and it publishes the bimonthly journal *Foreign Affairs*.

Foreign Policy Association (FPA)
470 Park Ave. S., 2nd Floor., New York, NY   10016
(212) 481-8100 • fax: (212) 481-9275
e-mail: info@fpa.org
Web site: www.fpa.org

FPA is a nonprofit organization that believes a concerned and informed public is the foundation for an effective foreign policy. Publications such as the annual *Great Decisions* briefing book and the quarterly Headline series review U.S. foreign policy issues in numerous countries, including Iran. FPA's Global Q & A series offers interviews with leading U.S. and foreign officials on issues concerning the Middle East, intelligence gathering, weapons of mass destruction, and military and diplomatic initiatives.

The Heritage Foundation
214 Massachusetts Ave. NE, Washington, DC   20002-4999
(202) 546-4400 • fax: (202) 546-8328
e-mail: info@heritage.org

Web site: www.heritage.org

The Heritage Foundation is a think tank that promotes conservative public policies, including a strong national defense. The foundation advocates a policy of aggressive diplomacy, plus a willingness to use force, to prevent Iran from becoming a nuclear power. Its Web site features an "Iran Briefing Room," tracking recent news about Iran, as well as numerous essays on the danger posed by that country.

Hoover Institution

Stanford University, Stanford, CA   94305-6010
(650) 723-1754 • fax: (877) 466-8374
Web site: www-hoover.stanford.edu

The Hoover Institution on War, Revolution and Peace at Stanford University is a conservative public policy research center devoted to advanced study of politics, economics, and international affairs. The institution hosts world-renowned scholars and ongoing programs of policy-oriented research. Its many publications include *Weekly Essays*, the quarterly *Hoover Digest*, and the bimonthly *Policy Review*.

National Council of Resistance of Iran

PO Box 2516, London   NW4 2DD UK
e-mail: info@ncr-iran.org
Web site: www.ncr-iran.org

The National Council of Resistance of Iran, a coalition of five Iranian political opposition organizations, bills itself as the parliament-in-exile of the Iranian Resistance. The council opposes the current Iranian regime and believes that Iran's nuclear program is more advanced and more of a danger than is commonly recognized. The council's publications include the weekly news bulletin *Iran Liberation* and the magazine *Lion and Sun*.

National Iranian American Council (NIAC)

c/o OAI, 2801 M St. NW, Washington, DC   20007
(202) 719-8071 • fax: (202) 719-8097
e-mail: info@niacouncil.org

Web site: www.niacouncil.org

NIAC is a nonpartisan, nonsectarian organization that promotes Iranian Americans' participation in American civic life. Fostering greater understanding between Iran and the United States is one of its stated goals. Its Web site includes an archive of news items about relations between Iran and the United States.

Nonproliferation Policy Education Center (NPEC)
1718 M St. NW, Suite 244, Washington, DC 20036
(202) 466-4406 • fax: (202) 659-5429
e-mail: npec@npec-web.org
Web site: www.npec-web.org

NPEC is dedicated to stopping the spread of strategic weapons, including nuclear, biological, and chemical weapons. The center advocates a more active U.S. nonproliferation policy and seeks to educate the press and academics about the dangers posed by weapons proliferation. Its publications include essays, reports, and the book *Getting Ready for a Nuclear-Ready Iran*.

Peace Action
1819 H St. NW, Suite 425, Washington, DC 20006
(202) 862-9740 • fax: (202) 862-9762
e-mail: paprog@igc.org
Web site: www.peace-action.org

Peace Action is a grassroots peace and justice organization that works for policy changes in Congress and the United Nations as well as in state and city legislatures. The organization supports a nuclear weapons–free zone in the Middle East and has called on the U.S. government to negotiate with both Iran and Israel to abandon their respective nuclear programs. Peace Action produces a quarterly newsletter and also publishes an annual voting record for members of Congress as well as numerous fact sheets.

U.S. Department of State
2201 C St. NW, Washington, DC 20520
Web site: www.state.gov

The State Department is a federal agency that advises the president on the formulation and execution of foreign policy. Congressional testimony and speeches given by State Department officials about Iran are available on its Web site.

Bibliography

Books

Geneive Abdo and Jonathan Lyons

Answering Only to God: Faith and Freedom in Twenty-First-Century Iran. New York: John Macrae, 2003.

William O. Beeman

The "Great Satan" v. the "Mad Mullahs": How the United States and Iran Demonize Each Other. Westport, CT: Praeger, 2005.

Christopher de Bellaigue

In the Rose Garden of the Martyrs: A Memoir of Iran. New York: HarperCollins, 2005.

Peter Brookes

A Devil's Triangle: Terrorism, Weapons of Mass Destruction, and Rogue States. Lanham, MD: Rowman & Littlefield, 2005.

Patrick Clawson and Michael Rubin

Eternal Iran: Continuity and Chaos. New York: Palgrave Macmillan, 2005.

Jerome R. Corsi

Atomic Iran: How the Terrorist Regime Bought the Bomb and American Politicians. Nashville, TN: WND, 2005.

David Frum and Richard Perle

An End to Evil: How to Win the War on Terror. New York: Random House, 2003.

Dilip Hiro

The Iranian Labyrinth: Journeys Through Theocratic Iran and Its Furies. New York: Nation, 2005.

Michael A. Ledeen	*The War Against the Terror Masters: Why It Happened, Where We Are Now, How We'll Win.* New York: St. Martin's, 2002.
Afshin Molavi	*Persian Pilgrimages: Journeys Across Iran.* New York: Norton, 2002.
Afshin Molavi	*The Soul of Iran: A Nation's Journey to Freedom.* New York: Norton, 2005.
Kenneth M. Pollack	*The Persian Puzzle: The Conflict Between Iran and America.* New York: Random House, 2004.
Elaine Sciolino	*Persian Mirrors: The Elusive Face of Iran.* New York: Free Press, 2001.
Henry Sokolski and Patrick Clawson, eds.	*Getting Ready for a Nuclear-Ready Iran.* Carlisle, PA: Strategic Studies Institute of the U.S. Army War College, 2005.
Kenneth R. Timmerman	*Countdown to Crisis: The Coming Nuclear Showdown with Iran.* New York: Crown Forum, 2005.
Robin Wright	*The Last Great Revolution: Turmoil and Transformation in Iran.* New York: Vintage, 2001.

Periodicals

Timothy Garton Ash	"Let's Make Sure We Do Better with Iran than We Did with Iraq," *Guardian* (Manchester, UK), January 12, 2006.
Reza Aslan	"Misunderstanding Iran," *Nation*, February 28, 2005.

Christopher de Bellaigue

"Iran," *Foreign Policy*, May/June 2005.

Jack Boureston and Charles D. Ferguson

"Keep Your Enemy Closer," *Bulletin of the Atomic Scientists*, November/December 2005.

Christopher Dickey, Maziar Bahari, and Babak Dehghanpisheh

"Iran's Rogue Rage: Nukes: Iranians Want Nuclear Know-How—and Seem to Be Daring the West to Stop Them," *Newsweek*, January 23, 2006.

Economist

"Still Not Blinking: Iran and the World," December 24, 2005.

Economist

"When the Soft Talk Has to Stop," January 14, 2006.

Robert J. Einhorn

"A Transatlantic Strategy on Iran's Nuclear Program," *Washington Quarterly*, Fall 2004.

Richard Ernsberger Jr., Ladane Nasseri, and Alan Isenberg

"Religion Versus Reality: Who Is This Man—a Mystic, a Bumbling Political Novice or an Imminent Threat to Iran's Established Order?" *Newsweek International*, December 12, 2005.

James Fallows

"Will Iran Be Next? Soldiers, Spies, and Diplomats Conduct a Classic Pentagon War Game—with Sobering Results," *Atlantic Monthly*, December 2004.

Robert O. Freedman

"Israel and the Threat from Iran's Nuclear Program," *Midstream*, March/April 2005.

Robert O. Freedman

"Soldiers of the Hidden Imam," *New York Review of Books*, vol. 52, no. 17, 2005.

Jeffrey Gedmin   "Plan B for Iran: Dealing with
                      President Ahmadinejad," *Weekly
                      Standard*, July 18, 2005.

Allister Heath   "A Monster of Our Own Making,"
                      Spectator, February 11, 2006.

Terrence Henry   "Nuclear Iran," *Atlantic Monthly*,
                      December 2003.

Lawrence F.   "Tehran Twist: Bush's New Iran
Kaplan   Policy," *New Republic*, March 28,
                      2005.

John Keegan   "We Should Be Very Worried About
                      Iran," *Daily Telegraph* (London),
                      January 12, 2006.

Joe Klein   "Shadow Land: Who's Winning the
                      Fight for Iran's Future?" *New Yorker*,
                      February 18, 2002.

Michael J. Mazar   "Strike Out: Attacking Iran Is a Bad
                      Idea," *New Republic*, August 15, 2005.

Fariborz   "No One Will Scratch My Back:
Mokhtari   Iranian Security Perceptions in
                      Historical Context," *Middle East
                      Journal*, Spring 2005.

Afshin Molavi   "Buying Time in Tehran—Iran and
                      the China Model," *Foreign Affairs*,
                      November/December 2004.

Scott Peterson   "Iran's Leader Drawing Fire,"
                      Christian Science Monitor, December
                      12, 2005.

Kenneth Pollack   "Taking on Tehran," *Foreign Affairs*,
and Ray Takeyh   March/April 2005.

Edward T. Pound   "Special Report: The Iran Connec-
and Jennifer Jack   tion," *U.S. News & World Report*,
                      November 22, 2004.

R. K. Ramazani — "Ideology and Pragmatism in Iran's Foreign Policy," *Middle East Journal*, Fall 2004.

Karim Sadjadpour — "Iranians Don't Want to Go Nuclear," *Washington Post*, February 3, 2004.

Richard Seymour — "With Us or Against Us—Iran Talks Tough," *Middle East*, February 2006.

Henry Sokolski — "Defusing Iran's Bomb," *Policy Review*, June/July 2005.

Steven R. Ward — "The Continuing Evolution of Iran's Military Doctrine," *Middle East Journal*, Fall 2005.

Fareed Zakaria — "Time to Face Reality on Iran," *Newsweek*, January 30, 2006.

Glossary

Mahmoud Ahmadinejad (last name may also be spelled Ahmadi Nezhad or Ahmadi-Nezhad) President of Iran since August 3, 2005.

Ansar al-Islam An Islamic terrorist group operating in Iraq and supported by Iran; its name translates as "Supporters of Islam."

Basij A volunteer militia within Iran's Islamic Revolutionary Guard Corps that is responsible for, among other things, enforcing Islamic law.

Mohamed ElBaradei Director general of the International Atomic Energy Agency.

Farsi (also known as Persian) The language spoken in Iran.

Hizballah (may also be spelled Hezbollah) An Islamic political party/militant group based in Lebanon and founded in the early 1980s with Iran's support; its name translates as "Party of God."

International Atomic Energy Agency (IAEA) The agency of the United Nations in charge of promoting the peaceful, safe use of nuclear energy and stopping the spread of nuclear weapons.

Islamic Revolutionary Guard Corps (also known as the Pasdaran) A separate Iranian army charged with protecting and enforcing the Islamic Revolution; it operates parallel to the regular army, which is responsible for protecting Iranian territory.

Ayatollah Ali Khamenei President of Iran, 1981–1989; as Iran's leading cleric, he has held the title of supreme leader of Iran since 1989.

A(bdul) Q(adeer) Khan Pakistani engineer who secretly shared nuclear technology with several countries, including Iran, Libya, and North Korea.

Mohammad Khatami President of Iran, 1997–August 3, 2005.

Ayatollah Ruhollah Khomeini Spiritual leader of the Islamic Revolution; supreme leader of Iran, 1979–1989.

Majlis (may also be spelled Majles) The Iranian parliament.

Nuclear Non-Proliferation Treaty (NPT) A 1968 international treaty, signed by the vast majority of the countries of the world, in which countries that do not have nuclear weapons agree not to seek them and the five countries that had nuclear weapons when the treaty was written agree not to spread their nuclear weapons technology to other countries.

Osirak (may also be spelled Osiraq) An Iraqi nuclear plant that was destroyed by the Israeli air force in a surprise attack in 1981.

Pasdaran *See* Islamic Revolutionary Guard Corps.

Ali Akbar Hashemi Rafsanjani President of Iran, 1989–1997.

shah The Iranian title for a king or emperor.

Grand Ayatollah Ali al-Sistani Iranian-born supreme religious leader of Iraq's Shiite community.

Tehran (may also be spelled Teheran) The capital of Iran.

Index